Shifting Gears

Copyright © 2017 by Changing Lanes International
All rights reserved. This book or any portion thereof may not be reproduced or used in any manner whatsoever without the express written permission of the publisher except for the use of brief quotations in a book review.

Printed in the United States of America

Shifting Gears, printed 2017

ISBN-13: 978-1979157360
ISBN-10: 1979157367

Changing Lanes International
www.changinglanesinternational.com

PROLOGUE

The road to success is always under construction.

When life changes, and it inevitably does every day, it is our ability to adapt swiftly that determines where our path will lead. In the end, it's not the places we have been that matter but those we have yet to experience that determine our destiny.

Success is often only one exit away. However, most people get off too soon and never fully experience what the roads less traveled could truly afford them.

During our journey, objects in our mirrors may be closer than appear, but on the road of life, our dreams often seem distant and nearly unreachable.

Yet, for those who are willing to shift gears and turbocharge their lives and accelerate their dreams, there is an open super highway paved with anything and everything you can imagine and desire.

The true Lane Changers are those who keep driving forward until they reach the intersection of purpose and passion, combined with their ultimate skill set and consistent, massive action. Once you reach that destination, the road ahead becomes so clear, resulting in a joy ride filled with unimaginable experiences and blessings.

While the road to success is never smooth, it is ours to pave. Go the extra mile and be bold on the boulevard of to your dreams.

The challenge becomes when you are at a crossroads or stuck in a lane that is not serving you personally and professionally, how do you Change Lanes?

There is a high road and a low road. There are a few who are on the high road who do whatever it takes to get and stay there.

The fears we don't face become our limits.

Lane Changers know the greater the change, the greater the joy.

When it comes to choosing a lane, most take a back seat to what they truly want and settle for what they accept, which is far less than their capability.

Some people waste their whole life because they are so afraid to live it. Some people live their whole life because they are so afraid to waste it.

Life isn't about where you start or end, it's all about the distance in between.

The fear of failure is the roadblock to your dreams.

Sometimes life puts you on a path you didn't want to be on but somehow at the end of the path there's opportunity there that you would have never discovered.

When you face obstacles in life, don't ask "why me?", instead hold your head high and say "try me."

You hold the wheel that will direct your ultimate destiny.

If everything seems under control, you're not going fast enough. Most of us have gears we never use.

If you can still hear your fears, it's time to shift gears.

This is your turn to Shift Gears, get revved up about your future, turbocharge your purpose and bypass a good life on your way to a great life.
Let's change gears and let's go full throttle together.

Kevin Harrington,
Inventor of the infomercial, original Shark on Shark Tank, and Pioneer of the "As Seen On TV" Industry

ENCOURAGEMENT FROM THE AUTHOR

When I thought I was at the end, and didn't know how to make ends meet, is when God met me where I was and changed the road I was traveling to pave a better future for myself, and so many others. When I had no belongings and didn't feel like I belonged, getting turned down over and over and turning over and over in my sleep, never feeling alive, so broke the only thing I could do was pay attention, nevertheless never giving up and never feeling fully broken; when hope was the only thing that held my attention, I was hopeless overall, but always focused on the glimmer of faith - even when I ran out of money, I was running on desire, and adjusted my sight from my lack of resources to the ability to be resourceful. I was so far from where I wanted to be but closer than I was before I started down the road to greatness - pressing on when my results were depressing, knowing I wasn't growing but still going forward, showing up, and not slowing down, I Changed Lanes, changed my life and have a mission of shifting the lives of others because the only thing in my life that has remained permanent is change.

I became hungry for success, eating up all the personal development and knowledge from mentors I could, getting overloaded on wisdom while getting the skinny on achievement. You see today I couldn't see what I was blind to then and soon I won't know what I was blind to now, but now it's not my sight that leads me but my vision. The road ahead seems brighter because of the headlights that lead the path paved only by faith, hope and love, cemented in my soul that I'm capable of everything...and it appears more concrete that it's imperative now, more than ever, to grab the wheel and drive the world forward, not because I can, but because so many others think they cannot.

You see, we are the windshield for those who will remain stuck in a rut looking through their rear view reflecting on all the problems instead of at the solutions reflecting back at them in that proverbial life mirror. Ultimately, their shattering self-infliction drives them toward the speed bumps they unconsciously construct, leading toward inevitable dead ends.

The only speed limit that completely stops us is the one we self-impose.

Conceivably, we can become impervious to our own incapacitating driver's manual that we have followed to get us here. For many, I adamantly believe they want to take the easy road to happiness, but don't realize there are no shortcuts to any place worth going. I would rather be on the rocky road to the success than the boulevard of broken dreams. Mile markers are flying by and the speed of life is accelerating rapidly; we cannot yield to our fears and we must stop at nothing to accomplish what we can hardly fathom is conceivable, because then we can go to unimaginable destinations, many of which are off the beaten path and lead to indescribable places.

Life is a journey and until I'm in a hearse, I'm going to put the pedal to the medal no matter how much it hurts because the pain is not in the achievement of the victory but in the failure of exiting before our greatest fulfillment. Live full and die empty. Set your GPS to the beginning of your best new life and shift your clutch to full throttle, reversing your poor habits and parking your fears in a vacant lot because you have a lot more to do to change the world in only the way you can.

Your dreams are closer than they appear, Lane Changer!!

Your Road. Your Dreams. Your Life.
Always Revved Up,
Lane Ethridge

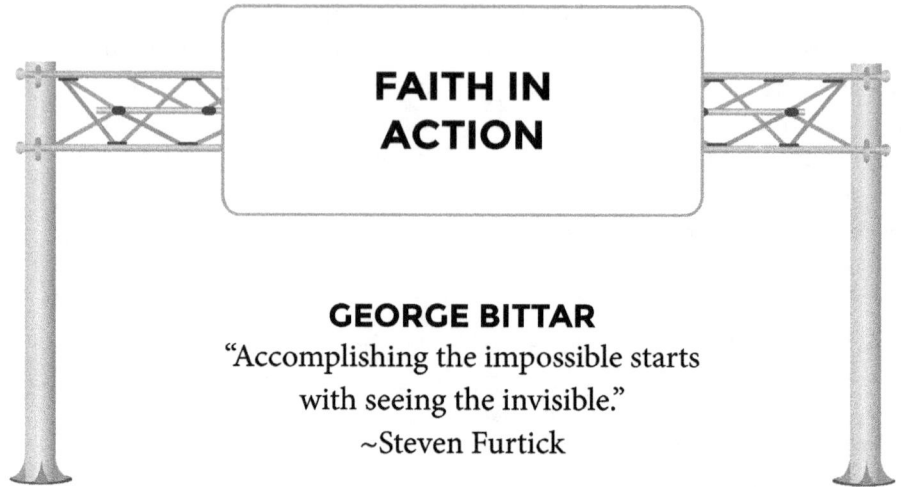

FAITH IN ACTION

GEORGE BITTAR
"Accomplishing the impossible starts
with seeing the invisible."
~Steven Furtick

Faith combined with action creates imposing transformation and since faith is ever flowing, when we remain stagnant, we thwart God's possible favor in our lives. Ultimately, it becomes not something we believe, but something we live. Even when the road ahead appears dark, we must keep moving forward.

George Bittar grew up in two households from a very young age, as his parents were separated by his first birthday. So young, he didn't really know anything different and realized that we only know what we are exposed to. Despite the perpetual love and support from his family, he started comparing himself to other kids and began understanding his insecurities as he got older. Both parents remarried and while he was close to his step-parents, he couldn't fully understand the dynamics of the different relationships and events he witnessed both good and bad. Because as a child many things are out of your control, George sought an escape out of disruptive environments. Spending the weekends with his father brought to light the dichotomy between his contrasting worlds. "These events start to condition and prep your mind, how you view the world and they become the foundation for your life," George proposes.

Over time, like George discovered the light and dark in his two worlds, his mother was introduced to the Lord and realized the true source of light and grace. While she faced many challenges, her sense of purpose and vision for her life enriched as she drew near to God's word. The positive changes in her life provided hope and encouragement for George and his siblings to aspire for healthy and hopeful lives.

We tend to become like those whom we admire. Children learn more from what you are than what you teach; they are great imitators so it is vital they have something great to emulate. Perhaps each of us should be the role models we needed when we were younger.

George developed an old soul mentality and always looked ten steps ahead during his adolescence. He surrounded himself with different groups of friends who didn't make the best decisions and influenced many of his choices. While they lived for today and always pushing the envelope, George had his limits and something always preserved him to only go so far and not end up abandoning school, getting in trouble with the law and perhaps even worst outcomes that others found themselves in. George suspended his beliefs that he should be like those who he wanted to avoid. He started thinking about his future and wanting to create a positive life of value and contribution. It became the renewing of his mind that repurposed his direction and desire for a better way.

As he grew older, he started learning from those around him who were wiser. His grandparents and family had fled Cuba under the Castro regime, leaving all their assets, belongings and entire life behind and arriving in the United States essentially with nothing. His grandfather was an uninterrupted innovator and started a family business that provided for them in the U.S. Following high school George struggled with his college courses and realized that it was not the right path for him at the time. An entrepreneur at heart, he went to work for his grandfather's family business in hopes to one day run it completely. Eventually, his grandfather was ready to sell the business and while George wanted to take it over, his grandfather didn't feel he was ready for that responsibility. Heartbroken, questioning his self-worth, hope on the road to success as an entrepreneur took a wrong turn and he wound up on the boulevard of broken hopes and dreams.

With no real clear path, George had dropped out of college, was newly unemployed and was not sure how things would come around again.

Do you turn right when you have nothing left or turn left when nothing seems to be going right?

The reality is that you never know how strong you can be until a curve in the road throws you into uncharted territory.

The hardest part of beginning again, is beginning.

Seeking a new lane to travel, George was introduced to an opportunity with a mortgage company. While it was his first experience in the corporate world and he had envisioned himself only working in an office that he owned, he was frustrated, but at least had a direction to go.

Sometimes life puts you on a path you didn't want to be on, but somehow at the end of the path there is opportunity there that you would have never discovered.

When you face obstacles in life, don't ask 'Why me?', instead hold your head high and say 'Try me!'

The fear of failure is the roadblock to your ultimate potential.

George overcame the hostility toward the new chance life provided. The position at the company afforded him a mentor and the mortgage industry became the vehicle George would use to drive his success over the last 20 years.

While he got off to a fast start, he discovered the sales guys were making 5-figure monthly checks and they were more in the flow of what he wanted. They were building out their own destiny. George continued to have strong work ethic and made great connections. One thing led to another and he ended earning a promotion in the sales department.

While the mortgage industry was booming and was downhill for experienced loan officers, it was uphill right away for George, learning tough lessons that served him well throughout his journey.

His first day in sales, his manager approached him to assess his results for the day. It was 7pm and George had been there since 9am cold calling for new business because he wasn't on rotation yet for live customer leads. Inquiring on how many deals he had closed, George responded that he had made a lot of calls and set up some appointments from his list, hopeful he would get something in the next couple days. With a harsh response due to the fact George didn't have anything for the day, albeit his first, his manager suggested he go home and consider if this position was really for him. "It's like someone punched me in the stomach and knocked the life out of me."

In sales, if you can't stomach the truth, you will wind up at a dead end with no money.

To make things more difficult, one of his coworkers informed George his cubicle had never had anyone succeed in it. Everyone before him had either been fired or not closed enough deals to survive. "It messed with my mindset a little bit, but I was confident in myself. The next morning, I came in early to pray and speak life over my cubicle. I needed to visualize positive outcomes in my heart, mind and spirit and to reverse the trend of past employees that sat in my seat and did not make it."

He affirmed his success and quickly had massive results. He made victory concrete in his mind and heart and began paving a path with earnest faith and devout dedication to his results.

In the end, a straight path does not make a skilled driver and you cannot break records with your foot on the brake. He continued to perfect his craft and out work everyone on the team. "I found my own way and was able to turn things around and experience ultra-success." In his first year, George qualified for Presidents Club, an elite and exclusive accomplishment for top producers. When he received his award on stage and enjoyed an all-expense paid trip for his achievement, he thanked God for the many blessings and favors.

It appeared that each mile marker on his road to success fueled his passion even greater.

He continued to thrive and had his most successful month ever.

But eventually things took a turn and he hit a plateau.

"I think I got comfortable and things just weren't working. My pride was suffering and I couldn't find my way back," George remembers.

One bad month led to another and he was put on final warning by management, specifically his new manager, Greg, who had just taken over his team. While it was difficult to hear, George feels indebted to Greg for fighting for him. George's accolades and reputation had preceded him and his new manager believed in him when others didn't, even when George didn't believe in himself. Through his favor and mercy, Greg fought for him when others were fighting to have him fired. His renewed faith in himself fired him up and George believed it was God's answered prayer and blessing in the cubicle he had asked for blessings on earlier in his career.

How do you respond when life gives us an obvious signal?

We often ask for signs but just speed right by them because we don't think they apply to us even though we asked for them.

Greg, wanting George to succeed so badly, enabled access to a company laptop at home so he could continue prospecting and closing deals to stay on the team. George took his efforts into overdrive and worked while others took breaks. He created a plan and worked the plan. Quickly after, he got off the warning list and three months later he was promoted to sales manager.

"I learned how to deal with challenges and get through obstacles. I realized I couldn't do everything by my own ability," George concedes.

Sometimes our own efforts can only take us so far, especially when things are out of our control.

George was at a crossroads when the mortgage industry dried up along with the real estate crash that came with little warning. Meanwhile, he was also experiencing a collapse in his personal life. Separated and eventually divorced, everything he banked on was upside down, including his relationship with the Lord.

With no genuine backup plan and dealing with a lot of turmoil and stress, he found his way into banking.

Hired as a branch manager with no prior experience, George trusts it was God's favor in his life. Ultimately, we can make deposits into our banks, but it's the investment others make into us that pays the highest dividend. We can never repay a debt we don't owe but we should always know that the ultimate price has already been paid. Because of that, our lives are always valuable and our journey always priceless.

With the restoration of a new marriage and two beautiful children, George aspires to provide for his family and experience all of God's promises.

He especially yearns for more when it comes to his personal growth and pursuing his passion.

He used to look at his cubicle as freedom from his old life and now views it as a prison confining him from the freedom he knows he can create as business person and entrepreneur.

The entrepreneurial drive he gained from his grandfather continues to fuel his life and desire to pursue his dreams.

"I had this urge to prime myself leading into my 40th birthday and really begin to condition myself and reflect back on the things that haven't gone well, as well as those things I knew were important to me that I haven't done. I had to get honest with myself and I used the opportunity to get motivated to not waste any more time. I started to picture myself hitting on all cylinders. I've just kind of been getting by dealing with whatever life throws at me and I don't want to live that way. We need to live intentional lives. God didn't put us on this Earth to just work, pay bills and die. Life is so much greater than that," George craves.

With a longing for so much more, feeling fully engaged, George found the courage to pull the trigger on his first real estate investment. While he has one foot safely in the corporate world, he has the other dipping into real estate investing and establishing additional streams. While his new investment property was settling, George unfortunately settled, too. His small successes satisfied him enough but part of him knew that he is capable of so much more.

Often, we don't have to be better than everyone else, we just have to believe we can be better than we ever thought possible. To reach our greatest destinations, however, we often have to fight our greatest fears.

There are countless ways of achieving greatness, but any road to achieving one's maximum potential must be built on the highway of unwavering belief and commitment.

George continues to drive toward a term he heard recently- becoming a "whole-life millionaire", which is a life fully balanced spiritually, relationally, physically and financially. "I'm still on the journey and now it's about scaling. Long term, I want to call my own shots."

Through live visualization, prayer and affirmations, he continues to project himself into the life he wants to create.

"I'm learning to trust God even more. I don't want to forget about the things God has put in my heart and know that I was created to do more. While the financial services industry has been good to me, I know I need to make that pivot out of the corporate world and put together a formula to help others that are frustrated do the same."

Some people waste their whole life because they are so afraid to live it; others live their whole life because they are so afraid to waste it.

Life isn't about where you start or end, it's about the distance in between.

And it's about the people along the way.

Life is not meant to be traveled alone.

George credits a lot of his life's direction to his parents, specifically his mother, who was indirectly affected by her cousin who brought her to the Lord. Watching his mom conquer her challenges – relationally, financially and even a life threating disease - created a shift for George. Her redirect served as a catalyst for his lane change. She has always been a visionary, keeping the faith, turning the impossible into the improbable and ultimately into the inevitable. His father has always been by his side despite living in separate households and has always put his children first showing unwavering, unconditional love no matter what they are facing. His father has had to handle his own adversity and always thrived on a positive attitude, never giving up and working hard to figure out solutions instead of focusing on problems.

There are times when God gives us mountains simply to show others they can be moved.

Success favors those who go after everything they want. When you play all out, things will always play out in your favor.

Prayer has served as his steering wheel whereas it used to serve as his spare tire.

"I'm going to rely on God more continually, not just when I hit those bumps in the road."

Every problem has a solution. Sometimes it may take longer than others but when you are going through adversity, being able to face it and put a plan around it creates alignment to keep driving ahead. At times, emotions may overwhelm you to the point of inaction. There may be times when you need to remove the feelings and just simply take massive, uninterrupted action.

Redirecting our focus to our past achievements, who we are as a result and what we have accomplished, becomes the proof that we have what it takes to go out and do even more! It's paramount that we don't compare our weaknesses to someone else's strengths. We cannot live positive lives with negative minds. When we shift our perspective and change the way we look at things, the things we look at change.

Limited beliefs create an upper limit to our potential. The best GPS along the road to success is a driver's manual with directions based on an unrelenting, unlimited and infinite mindset. And the more jubilant the journey the more likely life will be a joy ride. When you allow passion to be the driving force and follow closely behind your values, the road will open to exceptional possibilities and favor. For George, his ambitiousness, commitment and ability to develop others, has helped him lead his life and enthuse others to live their lives more inspired.

While George had dropped out of college because it wasn't the right lane for him at the time, through his company's financial support he was able to pursue his degree once again and have it almost fully funded. Not only did he graduate, he did so with honors. When he walked across the stage to receive his diploma, while he felt a huge sense of satisfaction through his accomplishment, it was the model he set for his family that made him most proud. While the journey wasn't always the most exciting, he kept the end in mind and was committed to the goal to show them that anything is possible with hard work and devotion.

Through creative resourcefulness, intentional risk, effective execution, consistent persistence and failing forward faster, George has excelled in the many lanes he has traveled.

Empowered leaders get revved up by empowering others. Frontrunners understand that the speed of the leader determines the speed of the pack. In principle, their forward progress allows others to draft off their momentum and experience stimulating breakthroughs that afford them an even greater sense of fulfillment.

Learning how to cope with setbacks sets us up for even greater comebacks. Failure is inevitable but success is a choice. Throughout life, our circumstances change as do our priorities. With a humbling approach to life, while George is creating many avenues of income for his family, his true excitement comes from living in perfect peace every day, fully harmonious with his God-given talents and calling.

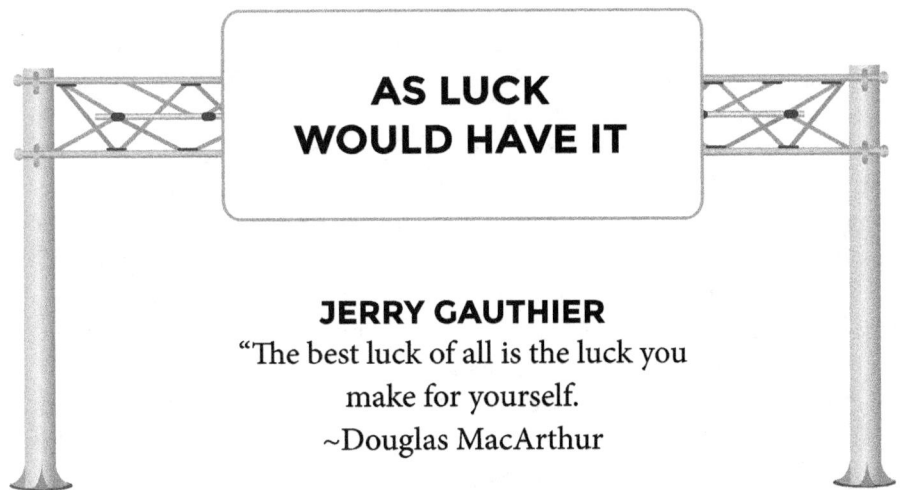

AS LUCK WOULD HAVE IT

JERRY GAUTHIER
"The best luck of all is the luck you
make for yourself.
~Douglas MacArthur

You may not always end up where you thought you were going but you will always end up where you were meant to be. When you outwork everyone, the world will work in your favor because success favors those on the intersection of preparation and opportunity. We all have future inevitabilities, we just need to drive forward long enough until they we catch them. Ultimately, fate doesn't ask you what you want because it knows what's best even when you don't. Sometimes we get lucky on the road we elect to take while other times we meet our fate on the road we take to avoid it. We can wish it and want it, but we must work for it and sometimes not getting what we want becomes a wonderful stroke of luck.

Born in Rockaway, New Jersey, a blue collar town, Jerry Gauthier's father was in the Army and worked at the rock quarry while his mother worked multiples positions within a local bar. Both worked extremely hard to provide for the family and, as a result, Jerry and his brother incurred many responsibilities around the house. Additionally, because of the lack of resources, they were often resolute, constantly resourceful, creating what they needed from what they had. The beauty of this was that hard work was instilled in them as kids, which served Jerry well as he grew and developed as a man and a businessman.

One of the biggest events that impacted Jerry's life was a distressing incident playing outside with his brother at age 6. Playing in the back yard, unintentionally, a tree branch they were climbing snapped back and caught Jerry in the eye, essentially blinding him. His vision became blurred similar to swimming under water without goggles. Over the next 18 months he had 12 surgeries, and was forced to wear an eye patch for a year in first grade. Teased and badgered, his eyes were sensitive to the light and he became sensitive, practically numb and irate, eager to prove wrong other's insults and harassment.

Ultimately, much of his negative childhood experiences stem from that unfortunate occurrence with that tree branch, but even more positively, he grew solid personal roots because of his tough-it-out kind of upbringing and impactful family tree.

Jerry remembers his father teaching him lessons that at the time appeared harsh, but were firmly establishing many of the positive characteristics that would serve him as he matured. Specifically, one day in the back yard with his dad during the summer in 3rd grade, his father advocated that if he wasn't playing a sport he was going to get a job next year. Perplexed and curious about the reality of his dad's proclamation, he signed up to play football that next Fall. "I remember always trying to compete hard with my friends. My best friend was extremely athletic and I hated him beating me so I always worked extra hard. With my vision, I had to work even harder. I was developing this mentality and work ethic that would later resurface in a different form in my professional career," Jerry acknowledges.

In the classroom, his grades were average at best. On the field, any arena he entered, his performance was always second to none.

In due course, he attended college because he thought the traditional path was expected of him. He attended college for one year full time while working at the mall part time. Then he was presented an opportunity that would afford him the chance to shift gears. Offered a temp job at Hewlett Packard, Jerry took a full-time position with them and accepted the additional benefit of the company paying for his schooling. "This first Lane Change wasn't forced on me. I'm going to learn everything about my job and work harder than any of the guys in the field. I was never afraid of asking questions and sure enough a full-time permanent opportunity came up and I was the clear choice. I doubled down and worked twice as hard."

Jerry began seeing the realities of corporate America as he started having some success. Meanwhile, he started putting more effort into his schooling and started getting A's. He discovered the way you do one thing is the way you do everything. Motivated and exposed to the certainties of the company culture, Jerry's sense of responsibility escalated along with his ranks on the corporate ladder.

He was given more responsibilities and work benefits like uniforms, a computer and access to the corporate gym; for the first time he was gifted benefits and accesses not common the way it was growing up. Jerry showed his work ethic and was ultimately promoted from a temporary employee to a full time corporate employee in charge of his department. As he moved into being a site manager with a new firm, his sight changed from what was real to what was possible; his vision for his life started to gain clarity. He was eventually given a company car and a cell phone in addition to higher salary. Beyond the tangible stipends, he was given a title. For most, they will work for something, but for many they will die for recognition.

Despite all the blessings, Jerry recognized this wasn't the right lane for him and wanted to shift.

Many remain stuck in the lane with traffic they created because they are too afraid to change lanes due to the unknown roadblocks, speed bumps and potential potholes. Jerry admits to being nervous and afraid of changes, but knew changes were required to move in the direction he wanted to go.

This inevitability for Jerry created the perfect storm to change lanes. He knew that it was better to be in the correct lane rather than the wrong one that leads to an undesirable endpoint. When you follow your heart and trust the path, you will wind up on the road that leads you to the most beautiful destinations.

Jerry's friend had graduated college and entered the economic world as financial advisor. Confident it was a good fit for Jerry, his friend mandated he attend an opportunity meeting to learn more. Jerry immediately became sold on the potential, despite the hard road ahead. He studied for the necessary licenses and started wearing a suit and tie, a new style change for sure, conforming to a new domain.

Early in his career, sitting across the table from prospects older than him who had worked their entire lives to create savings he wanted them to entrust him with, Jerry doubted his abilities as a 22 year-old kid fresh out college who still lived with his mom and dad. Money and Finance felt right but this domain was not the right fit. To remain true to his calling, Jerry knew that this path was a starting point but needed to take a different route.

That feeling in the long run about becoming a financial professional became the vehicle that would drive Jerry to a life of abundance and prosperity.

He has always banked on his skills and work ethic and found himself in the banking industry at age 23. Within a 3 month period, Jerry found himself switching from financial planning to banking, breaking up with his college sweetheart and purchasing his grandmother's house with no real savings; Jerry trusted the process and knew that incessant with hard work he could create his own luck.

In his first year, he took it upon himself to master his craft and outwork the limit he had put on himself. "I cracked the whip and never sat still and just waited for the clock to run out for the day where I wasn't progressing myself in some way. I don't want to lose this opportunity so I need to get really good really fast." At the end of the first year, he made twice as much as he ever had before.

Sandwiched between two veterans, Jerry ate up all their knowledge. He didn't want to compete with them but rather leverage what they weren't willing to do. He wanted to learn from them rather than create competition so he would follow up on the leads they discarded. He would work when others weren't willing to put in the time. Saturdays became his workmate, grinding 50 out of 52 his first year, leveraging the prospects who worked corporate hours and could only talk on the weekends. He opened the most accounts on Saturday and he found desirable what others found detestable.

When you want to go places, sometimes you have to grind nonstop.

By the end, all the singles and doubles added up and he was the top rookie producer. The person who hired him went to bat for him and Jerry stepped up to the plate and swung for the fences. He created the playbook that worked for him and implemented the plan that would create the results he desired. Additionally, like any good performer, he listened to his coach.

He began winning people over and the sales rep he sat next to truly became his first mentor in his professional career. "I would not have made it without someone showing me the way. I was a willing and apt pupil, respectful of his time and always wanted to provide value back to him so he would want to help me."

Jerry kept stepping up to the plate and swinging.

Nonetheless, with all great success, life continues to throw us curve balls.

Despite all the success and contribution to the company, Jerry was let go from the organization due to unforeseen and unfortunate circumstances, much of which was out of his control. A CPA that often sent Jerry business had referred him a client who Jerry called constantly, but failed to get a hold of. The client and he played phone tag and never really connected about the loan, resulting in an incomplete file that remained motionless in his pipeline. His manager inquired about the file during their sales meeting and discovered they hadn't officially spoken in person or on the phone. In the end, the information he shared with his manager, despite never withholding anything, became his un-doing with the firm. The company had to let Jerry go because of new company policies based on prior unethical behavior of some other employees. This became a forced lane change that would serve as an invaluable lesson despite the money it cost him. "It was a cold band aid rip off. I took it pretty well because I knew I couldn't fight it. It didn't take me long to learn this would never happen to me again. I'm not going to let ignorance put me at risk and I won't forget you are extremely expendable in corporate America," Jerry convicts. "I was the prodigal son one day and the next I was forced to leave."

Jerry was sidelined in the game of life. Sometimes we need to accept what is, let go of what was and have faith in what will be. The only thing we can absolutely control is how we react to the things which are out of our control.

Concerned about the future and unsure of where his next check was coming from, Jerry trusted that he had made his own luck before and he would prevail because of the reputation he had built. He supposed that circumstances would remain fortuitous for him despite the unknown.

Shortly after, he received a phone call from an HR rep at the bank where he had just lost his job who directed him toward a position at a different lending institution. Jerry accepted her recommendation and the person he was referred to knew of him because of his stellar performance and upstanding character. "I think you need a little luck in your life but I don't think it's luck that falls on your lap, I think it's luck that you make."

With a new position of authority as a manager, Jerry adopted new responsibilities and demands. He wasn't just responsible for his own success but his teams. "It developed me so much that it changed the way I interacted with my friends and family. It really matured me because he now had a staff that looked to me as the captain calling the shots. Wrong or right I had to make a decision."

There are many squirrels splattered on roads because they couldn't make a decision and act quickly enough. There are many people in the business world who end up the same way because of their inability to decide and respond.

This was another situation where Jerry had to hit the reset button, relearn and repeat the cycle of success by being the first into the office and the last out. With many mergers and acquisitions, Jerry realized that success comes when hard work and enriched performance merge. He also discovered a key to his success when he was asked what direction he wanted his career to go. With a passion for a few different roles, he received advice from a mentor that would change everything for him. "You have to choose one and focus on it; you can't spread yourself all over the place because nobody is going to believe that you know what you want," she acclaimed.

If you can't buy into what you truly want, it will be nearly impossible to sell someone else on it, too.

"I gradually realized she was right," Jerry established. "More importantly, I realized I was wrong and it was a humbling effect that has happened time and time again in my career.

Naiveté and confidence can only take you so far. Many people go through life with knowledge on ice; many others go through life with ignorance on fire. The key, as Jerry has proved throughout many disciplines in the professional world, is that when you have knowledge on fire you can light up the record books.

Changing lanes many times while shifting constantly within his organizations, Jerry's drive was always in full gear. As he advanced and escalated to more significant positions, he discovered more about himself along the way. With a keen desire to do things his way, relying on his ability to perform, it was ultimately revealed to him that providence always prevails. While it took him years to identify the best lane for him, until it became clear and magnified undoubtedly, he never veered from reaching the pinnacle destination.

When he transitioned from the retail side of banking where he had exceled for a decade to the product specialty on a much bigger level, it was the most impactful lane change that would change him most pointedly. He went from managing people to managing other managers and opened an entire new dynamic. This became the first experience where he didn't have a mentor in this space and had to learn new systems in emerging markets that produced massive volume, forcing him to accelerate his performance. When you're put into an overwhelming role, you're either going to crash real fast or make it through, gaining the experience of what others take years to obtain. Jerry realized how lucky he was to have been gifted with the position in a rapidly advancing opportunity. While most become astounded and cripple in the face of adversity, Jerry thrived and produced twice as many transactions at considerably higher amounts than others. Along with his team's success, they went from 8th to number one in growth and it served as his number one personal growth experience.

When you want to speed up your success, sometimes you have to buckle down and grind even harder even when it's exceedingly exhausting.

Jerry did that consistently, until he got a break pursuing a new position in commercial lending.

Committed to his mission, even taking vacation days to shadow other commercial lenders to learn the ropes, Jerry understood the best ROI for him was betting on himself. "The bank wasn't giving me the shot in commercial lending because I didn't have the background, so I went out and paid for myself to go through the training". I kept at the job posting and essentially forced my way into an interview. When my now boss saw all that I was willing to do to get this lateral position, he gave me the chance," Jerry proclaims.

Despite not being formally credit trained through the bank's program, not having a finance/accounting degree and zero commercial lending experience, Jerry was extended a position reconfirming lucky people get opportunities, brave people create opportunities and winners are those who convert problems into opportunities.

This new position in the bank was double the distance away from home and the hours were going to be much longer with no overtime to make up for those additional hours. But at age 36, years behind his personal schedule, it was finally a foot in the door to where Jerry wanted to go.

Luck is not in your hands, but decision is in your hands. Your decisions can make luck but luck can never make your decision so always trust yourself. We can ask and seek, but luck happens when opportunity knocks and you answer.

"Tell me I can't do something or get something because I'm not good enough, I'll get good!" Jerry confidently admits. "It was a real lane change because I had to sacrifice so much more to get where I wanted to go. I knew if I could just get on the field I would get on the starting lineup." Our goals must remain out of reach but never out of sight. Throughout your journey, it's only partly how bad you want it and mostly how hard you're willing to work for it.

The intangible ability that's needed to acquire the palpable goals we strive for is not standard. The uncommon leaders who excel are those who obtain the necessary skill set and utilize it day in and day out with an unwavering commitment along with a consummate mindset. Not everybody is fortunate enough to be dealt the best hand but we are all capable of playing the hand we've been dealt and create our own fortune.

When you start out, to get up and running you may have to get down and dirty. The toughest part of getting to the top is getting through the crowd at the bottom. Getting to the top should be a priority, but being aware of why you want to stay there should be the focus.

Exposure to the best of the best exposes your weaknesses to become even stronger.

Jerry continues to have a sense of urgency to do better and prove to everyone, including himself, that when it comes to his career he doesn't want to just be middle of the road.

When you continue down the path to greatness, new roads open up. Leveraging his knowledge in banking, Jerry has ventured down other avenues and become a venture capitalist for businesses he believes in, namely one with his best friend who inspires his drive to perform even better. Together, founding and building Hotseat Warmers, they are paving a new way in the sports world with a product they created that they have currently sold to 5 NFL teams and a few collegiate sports teams. Despite the disbelief from those closest to them, they pushed through and started pulling in contracts, tackling obstacles and scoring big!

Life will pitch you opportunities but you have to step up to the plate. Winners do what losers don't. Do not be afraid to swing for the fences and remember that the small hits along the way will help you score, and provide others the ability to score also.

"It's been a long road to get here but I love my job and today it's everything and more than I ever thought. You don't get anywhere without major sacrifices and I'm so appreciative of where I am today because of all the hard work it took to get here. Shifting gears is taking a leap of faith and not always knowing what's on the other side. I've been humbled so many times and brought back down to Earth."

With all the success, Jerry remains grounded. Every big tree started as a tiny nut hat held its ground. Becoming blinded by the tree branch during his childhood indirectly created the vision for his life. His family roots served as the stability he needed to prevail during turbulent times and weather his storms. While we all grow in different directions, our roots remain as one when we support those who want to rise to new heights. With his massive success, he now thrives on planting seeds in the fertile soil of those who want to grow with him. His goal is to continue to build a business that provides protection for his family. While much of his success has come from going out on a limb, it shadows in comparison to what he still has to accomplish.

Shifting Gears

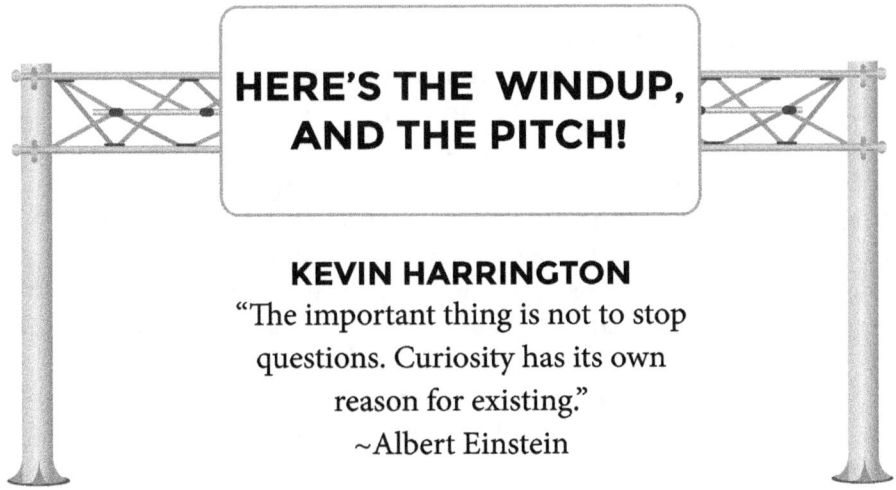

HERE'S THE WINDUP, AND THE PITCH!

KEVIN HARRINGTON

"The important thing is not to stop questions. Curiosity has its own reason for existing."
~Albert Einstein

Kevin Harrington has become a household name mostly by bringing a multitude of products from the marketplace into your home. The reality is that his success has come from taking advantage of life-changing experiences, seizing them and turning them into opportunities for others to create success. As one of the most successful entrepreneurs of our time, Kevin Harrington has taken over 500 products and businesses to the next level, generating more than $5 Billion in sales worldwide. And yet to reach this success, like all aspiring entrepreneurs, he had to start somewhere.

Kevin had the desire to own his own business and be an entrepreneur from a young age. And he understood that there is almost no such thing as ready. There is only now and as all successful business people, especially those who get into the fast lane, understand that now is as good a time as any. Grasping this concept, he began exposing himself and his persona to as many opportunities as possible. He entered what he calls the 'Curiosity Overload' phase in which he was on an exploration to figure out what he loved and where he could excel. "In life you have to present yourself and you have to focus on exposing yourself to more opportunities. The more opportunities you have, the bigger and better you can grow and build as an entrepreneur," Kevin adopts as a core principle.

Understanding he needed to acquire business savvy, at age 20, Kevin decided he would start a business brokerage business. While he didn't know everything he needed to create success, this endeavor forced him to comprehend the inner workings of dynamic businesses — why they were selling, why they were growing, why they were struggling and overall how these companies operated. Ultimately, Kevin uncovered key components that would later make him a fortune. "I was exposing myself through this 'curiosity overload' to many opportunities so that I knew when the right one came along that it was going to smack me in the face and send me the right direction."

Often, on the road of life we believe that we can just coast and it will all work out. If you don't know where you're going any road will get you there. Instead, professional entrepreneurs know that when we want to work things out in our favor, we pave the right lane for us and drive the world forward.

Kevin attended nearly every trade show to learn and emerge himself into the world he wanted to dominate. He would trade his time for knowledge and wisdom. When you study your competition, do what's necessary to learn the industry and do what it takes to create enough value in the marketplace, you will eventually surpass the competition. Today, Kevin continues to attend trade shows to fuel his 'curiosity overload,' stay in tune with new products and developing techniques, as well as expose himself to more opportunities and media. When we take the open road it will lead us to the best lane for us.

While Kevin was attending the Philadelphia Home Show, he observed a guy at a booth who was demonstrating the benefits of a ginsu knife, and more importantly he was successfully selling them. Observing that 9 out of 10 viewers would rush the table to purchase the knife set, the light bulb went off. "There's a guy that knows how to sell," Kevin noticed, "what if we put him up on television so that instead of being in front of 10 people he could be in front of millions?" Kevin invested $2000 into filming that presentation and eventually it turned into a $500 million program, Kevin had helped Arnold become a huge success. Arnold, seeing an opportunity himself, introduced Kevin to other pitch guys at various trade shows in exchange for a little piece of the action.

The birth of the infomercial impregnated a new market with life-changing products and Kevin became the father of an entire new industry that he created. Those who create dream lifestyles take an opportune moment and make it a momentous opportunity for others. The power of seizing and opportunity and creating leverage will take you from the slow lane to the fast lane! Life is about seizing those moments that could change everything you know. Change is constant and our lives need to change for us to be able to understand how to change more lives. When we look out for new beginnings, our outlook will be renewed and restored.

Many view Kevin's success as being lucky. "I programmed myself to be at the right place at the right time. I wanted to be in the right lane. I wanted to be in that fast lane to success. But you need to stay in the fast lane, that game-changing lane that gives you the ability to speed right through it all." As Kevin built his empire, he actually started with the finish line first. While he didn't know what vehicle would drive him to success, he knew the destination. On the journey, there is a road map and a set of directions. The first allows you options to arrive there any possible way while the latter gives you a specific course to navigate. As a revolutionary pioneer, Kevin used a map to create his set of directions. The counsel he has developed over time in his pursuit to becoming one of the most influential investors in today's market worldwide, Kevin became one of the original panelists on the hit TV show "Shark Tank." He shares his process to create a powerful and influential pitch whether you're making the sale of a product, attracting investors or getting a promotion:

1) Start with the problem in order to gain the listener's attention
2) Solve the problem using some magical transformations and benefits in a unique fashion
3) Make an irresistible offer

The entire concept is structured to Tease, Please and then Seize!!

And while most simply talk about what it takes, Kevin continues being curious while remaining furious, continually raises his profile and programs himself to become a person of influence and continuously tests before he invests. When you get into the right lane and you're accelerating, you have the opportunity to stay at the head of your pack. In the entrepreneurial lane you need to watch out for other drivers because it's fast and furious and by continuing to innovate, you solidify yourself as a key person of influence and limit the ability of your competition to catch up. Ultimately, what drives Kevin is building a future for his family. He has no desire to slow down. Every day is a new day to impact people's lives and help them achieve their dreams. "My eyes are visualizing what's happening through their eyes and it's an opportunity for me to help them get in the fast lane. Some people are chugging along at 25 MPH and if they just had my vision, they would move over into the fast lane and get there a lot faster," Kevin confirms.

At the end of the day, the things that happen to us are not as important as our attitude and perspective about those momentous opportunities in our lives. Life is about seizing those moments that could change everything you know. Yours will be marked by extraordinary defeats and even more extraordinary accomplishments. Those who create massive success take an opportune moment, seize the opportunity and make it a momentous opportunity for others. Then they take it into overdrive and accelerate their contribution to the world.

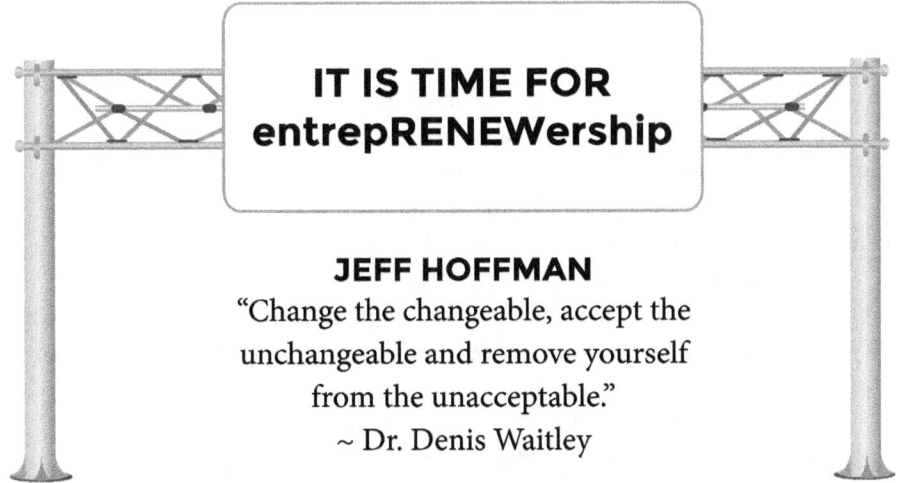

IT IS TIME FOR entrepRENEWership

JEFF HOFFMAN

"Change the changeable, accept the unchangeable and remove yourself from the unacceptable."
~ Dr. Denis Waitley

Jeff Hoffman is a world-leading entrepreneur with a vision that supersedes money and pays a far bigger dividend. Over the course of his career he has launched some of the most well-known start-up companies, and what began as a means to end turned into a new beginning that is changing the world.

Entrepreneurship for Jeff, like many, started unintentionally because he had a problem he couldn't solve; he wanted to attend a college he couldn't afford. Through scholarships and financial aid, he was able to attend but through lack of funds he was told to go home. And the average person would have. And the average entrepreneur when faced with a challenge quits too. But Jeff realized if he listened to everyone telling him to drop out and quit, that would have set his standard for the future.

As a freshman, Jeff started his first company simply to be able to fund his goal of receiving a college diploma. The real lesson was learned outside of academia. He quickly learned that if you have a hard problem to solve and nobody else to help you solve it, entrepreneurship and start-ups can serve as a great means to an end.

Throughout school we are taught a lesson and then given the test. In life, we are given a test and have to decipher the lesson. And along the traditional path, somebody's unwritten rule book dictates that we should go to school, get a degree that is supposed to serve the purpose of getting a job at good company.

And Jeff did just that.

Yet he hated every day of his corporate job because of the bureaucracy, the politics and the heavy overhead of constantly having to please management and not customers.

Like many, frustrated and challenged, Jeff simply wanted control of his own destiny. He needed a lane change

He realized that entrepreneurship was the vehicle that would open new lanes to freedom and self-determination. It was never about the money; it was about the choices he wanted to be able to design his own life.

Jeff discerns that the difference between entrepreneurs and everybody else is how we handle our problems. Recognizing that we all encounter difficulties in the world, entrepreneurs observe the problem and determine if it's bothering anybody else. If the answer is yes, they do research to determine if there is already a solution to the problem. And finally, if there is not a viable answer, they figure out the solution with a determinant attitude that they are the one who should be the solution to the problem.

"Inefficiency makes me nuts," Jeff recognizes, "and I have a singular focus of resolving a problem and I won't sleep until that thing is fixed."

Yet Jeff also recognizes that it's not a one-lane road. Each of us has something we do really well, but it's paramount to surround yourself with people who are smarter than you in the areas that you're weakest in. Jeff believes that while most people purport that the biggest need for start-ups is funding, talent is much more scare than money. He puts such a huge emphasis on networking and encourages entrepreneurs to always be searching for new talent to create collaboration. The strength of your network determines the strength of your team. And if you start searching for someone when you need them, you're already too far behind.

And sometimes within a company, there may need to be a change of roles to maximize the efficiency of the mission. While you may be educated in a particular niche, it may be a reality that there is someone within the company that is better than you. Jeff remembers first hand, while acting as the CEO, being called out and asked to change his contribution to the company. While his degree was in computer science and programming, the best role for Jeff was not programming because he wasn't the most proficient. And while that doesn't make you obsolete, it certainly makes you less impactful than that team member.

Ego aside, Jeff realized that in order to contribute the greatest to the overall mission, his role would be better for the company in marketing. While he didn't know marketing, he did research by interviewing marketers. He realized that they couldn't understand the engineering and technology side while the engineers couldn't communicate with the marketers in business terms. This was pivotal moment for Jeff, creating his most impactful lane change as an entrepreneur. He recognized a gap. Some people in his company were in the far left lane and some people were in the far right lane and nobody was in the center lane. Jeff made a shift and bridged the gap, creating a new position within the company and was able to drive the entire company forward and his career went into overdrive.

As a result of this radical shift, Jeff believes in both competition and collaboration. As a founder of Priceline.com and uBid.com, among others, he appreciates that there are components within a company where another company may be able to come alongside and collaborate. There could also be components within the same joint venture that competition will birth the best product. And even more possible is the idea that competitive collaboration will produce more wins for both companies.

Along the journey of self-discovery through building businesses, Jeff proposes that entrepreneurs are both born and made. There are a whole set of skills, tools, techniques and experiences that can be learned. There are also a lot of people who have made many mistakes and learned a lot of the lessons who can mentor you. That would suggest that anyone can become a successful entrepreneur. That said, fundamentally, there is a different mindset that determines the risk profile of someone and their ability, through unfiltered thinking, to create a solution from a problem.

Entrepreneurs thrive on uncertainty because it is an opportunity that stimulates them to get creative.

'Necessity is the mother of invention' and perhaps we could now suggest that 'uncertainty is the daddy of discovery and development.'

We find ourselves in an economic time that is fostering that need and desire for entrepreneurs. Through circumstance, people are discovering abilities they didn't tap into in order to create opportunities that aren't presently possible for them. Moreover, because of the huge tsunami of entrepreneurship, more opportunities are being created for people to evolve into entrepreneurs and adapt accordingly to create a new reality.

"Entrepreneurship is a privilege, not a job" Jeff suggests. The adventure that one goes on when choosing to accept the opportunity is more important than the money that comes with the success. Dreams can come true because of entrepreneurship. And entrepreneurs can also, more importantly, help the dreams of others become reality.

Jeff has transitioned from launching companies, to launching entrepreneurs who go launch new companies. The dollar that can be made by starting another company is not nearly as impactful as the difference that can be made by equipping an army of entrepreneurs to go change the world. Jeff determines who he wants to mentor based on their ability to scale and their amount of influence to pay it forward. When he believes that an entrepreneur will make a difference in the world based on their mission, he's more passionate about supporting their dreams.

As one of the founders of Priceline.com, Jeff admits that his passion for travel is really spawned by his love of people. He recognizes that the happiness index of a country is more important than the landmarks it can offer. His desire to learn about a country and its culture, along with the places where there is the most change in the air, are the places he loves visiting.

As the landscape of our world changes, so does that landscape of entrepreneurship. And so too, does that landscape of a man who has built some of the biggest companies that have shaped our world. When you get to enjoy the blessings that come with the hard work of finding a problem and creating a solution, life and business become more about the people behind the companies and the hearts and souls behind the vision. Entrepreneurship is the vehicle that can provide the solutions to the world's biggest challenges such as strife, war, political unrest and poverty. When you have nothing to lose and nothing to live for we resort to caring less about people. When you can teach others how to help themselves so they can create a better life, we can fundamentally resolve some of those conflicts.

Jeff is driven by the desire to show as many people the components of entrepreneurship. This will help create resolve in their own life so collectively we can resolve some of the biggest challenges we are facing throughout our world today. If we stay in the slow lane, we will stay stuck in a slow worldly demise. If we want to create a radical shift in the direction of our world, we need to get in the fast lane and pave the way via the road to entrepreneurship.

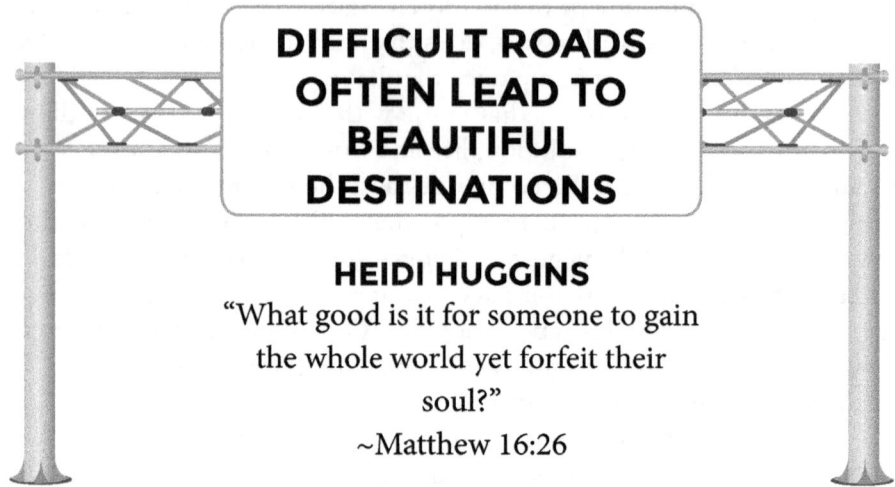

DIFFICULT ROADS OFTEN LEAD TO BEAUTIFUL DESTINATIONS

HEIDI HUGGINS

"What good is it for someone to gain the whole world yet forfeit their soul?"
~Matthew 16:26

    The key to living a life of abundance and love is learning to trust the journey even when you don't understand it all. There is unremitting brokenness, but until you're broken, you don't know what you're made of since struggle gives you the ability to create yourself all over again. Ultimately, no situation is too far gone for God to restore.

    Born in Ottawa Ontario, Canada as the first child of 4, Heidi Huggins was raised by her father, a police officer who drank often, and her mother, a loving and nurturing stay-at-home mom. When she was 5 years old she had an experience that shaped her childhood and would ultimately affect her adulthood because of its impactful magnitude. Playing in her front yard one day, Heidi was invited by a group of friends to go to the mall and she accepted, taking off without permission and crossing a 6-lane highway in the process. While at the shopping center, sitting under a department store chair, one of her friends who was seven, acted inappropriately toward Heidi and wanted her to reciprocate. Uncomfortable and confused at the time, Heidi didn't know how to respond. Later, Heidi understood that her friend was undoubtedly abused and the only outlet she knew was act accordingly.

    Nothing is weaker than the man who hurts women or children whether by his actions or by his words. In these situations, too many people stand back instead of stand up. Often, the scars we can't see are the hardest to heal.

When Heidi and the group of friends left the mall to head home, approaching a street light, the clique left Heidi behind and she was alone, physically and emotionally. An older man saw her and walked her across the highway, thankfully safely and promptly. In the end, she didn't fully know how to cope with the incident and blocked it out for most of her life. While she had felt abandoned, Heidi realized later that, despite the travesty of the experience, God was with her the entire time and anything could have happened.

Heidi felt loved by her family but became mostly withdrawn from other people. She wasn't completely down and out but at the same time she didn't really feel like she fit in.

Heidi's mother was always there for the kids but it was an unsafe atmosphere to truly thrive, to the point where her dad's drinking made all the kids anxious and unsure of what kind of mood he would be in. "My dad loved us but he had a funny way of showing it," Heidi evokes.

She attended a Christian school but felt withdrawn and never really fit in, and the kids constantly teased her boyish features, red hair and freckles. Insecure and emotional, when she was in junior high, Heidi began smoking and drinking. While school is supposed to be a place to be nurtured and supported, she had a difficult time learning and would get frustrated easily. She didn't feel smart and continually felt like an outcast, regularly feeling as if she were being separated and isolated.

In life, we sometimes think we want to disappear, but all we really want is to be found.

At the same time, not all who wander are lost.

No matter how alone we may feel, God who is always with us and will never abandon us or forsake us. And for our sake, we experience people coming and going from our lives to determine not who wants us in their lives, but who we want to accept into ours.

Yet, that may mean that we are attracted to people who we want to fill the void that only we can by allowing hope and faith through our Heavenly Father to enter in when we feel left out.

Heidi started dating guys who had deleterious influence on her and led her down destructive paths, paved with mal intent and self-seeking desires. We often turn to things for fulfillment when we are unfilled in our own insecurities. Eventually, Heidi began dating a guy twice her age and dropped out of high school, moved in with him and distanced herself from the family.

One day she borrowed his manual car, became distracted when she reached down to get the cigarettes that had fallen between the seats, and totaled the car when she crashed into a pole smashing her face almost unrecognizable.

To get the support she needed for her recovery, Heidi moved in with her grandparents and went back to school to get her diploma. Proud of her completion, despite her previous imprudent decision to drop out, she felt a sense of accomplishment that gave her a renewed self-worth and pride.

In challenging times, rather than distance ourselves from the things we don't want, we should draw near to the ones who can show us a restored route. The broken road of hardship is never the best path when you can take the one that leads you to grace and peace.

Heidi began working two jobs to make ends meet. "I was living for the moment and didn't really have any plans or goals for the future," she recognizes.

When we don't know where we are going, any road will take us there.

Shortly after, Heidi started dating a military guy who she had met on a blind date. She was blindsided when he moved back to Hawaii two days after their first date. Seven months after, she flew to Hawaii and married him. One year later after he got out of the Army, they moved back home and was pregnant with twins. Dreadfully, 5 months into the pregnancy they lost one of them. Their first son, Jacob was born with a skin condition they believe to have been contracted from his unborn brother. Eight months later Heidi became pregnant with their second son, Steven, while the marriage was becoming more challenging and intense. Her husband was gone a lot and Heidi discovered he had gotten involved in the porn industry, deceitful and untruthful about his reality. All the while, Heidi was unloved by her in laws while her husband would belittle her and verbally abuse her in public. She was caught in an unhealthy situation where she was verbally abused, but she put on a mask and thought it could actually be worse. She didn't know which way to go.

When we keep faith and keep driving forward, happiness is often found around bends in the road we never expected to turn.

Pregnant now with her third son, Eric, the hits just kept on coming. She fell during her first trimester and the doctor suggested there was only a 50 percent that he would survive because of the placenta abruption and hemorrhaging from the fall. On bed rest with a 1-and-2-year old, Heidi needed help that wasn't there from her husband. Thankfully, her sister-in-law was a home nurse and provided much needed support.

One and a half years later, Heidi became pregnant with Kenny. Due to the scar tissue that was created from the birth of Eric, Kenny's placenta latched onto the scar tissue and was not able to grow or develop normally. He was only 3.3 pounds at full-term. The doctors diagnosed him with biliary atresia, a rare liver disease, and were unsure if he would survive. The surgery he had to endure was portrayed to be a long 6 hours. Surprisingly, he was out of surgery in 1.5 hours and the doctors were astonished when they found no biliary atresia present. "We did a lot of praying before he went in for the procedure. We praise God because he truly is our miracle baby," Heidi praises. Kenny was able to go home 4 days later after being in the hospital for a month prior.

Heidi was such a proud mother but with all the contemptible behavior from her husband, feeling insecure and unappreciated despite getting in great shape to look more like the women in the porn industry, the tough road appeared to be never ending. Even the love for her children didn't provide her enough compassion and affection for her to hold on any longer.

She started getting attention from other guys and felt beautiful for the first time thanks to their adoration. In an act of infidelity, she acted on her unfamiliar affection. When she admitted her slip up to her husband, he forgave her and told her he didn't want her to leave because he wouldn't find another woman that looked like her. Heidi's looks mattered more to him than her heart. Although he never really showed it to her, he knew deep down he wouldn't find anyone as special as her.

We often start to appreciate what we think we will lose. Yet, often it's too late to hold onto something that had already slipped away long before as a result of our unmerited behavior.

They relocated to South Carolina in hopes of a fresh start, but the relationship was too putrid at that point.

In an attempt to feel love, Heidi found herself in an affair with their new neighbor shortly after relocating to South Carolina, in hopes to escape that exact unwholesomeness. She found herself pregnant while losing part of herself in the process. Devastated, she told the man she was having an affair with that it was her husband's and fused the relationship with him. Confused and living a lie, things spiraled out of control. She put her husband on the birth certificate because she wanted to protect her children. Shortly after, her son's actual father died from cardiac failure and Heidi's heart was torn as well.

Attending his funeral, she wanted to put her unhealthy way of life to death, too.

Heidi wore a proverbial scarlet letter and in unison, wore her heart on her sleeve.

But she didn't always have sleeves on to adorn her heart.

She wound up waitressing at a strip club and eventually became an exotic dancer. To escape her situation and not remain dependent on her husband, doing whatever it took despite the exposure, she put herself in a position that made her fully vulnerable. "The more money I made, the freer I felt," Heidi sheepishly accepts. The more money she made the closer it was to getting her own place and getting out from underneath her situation.

She was getting paid and being paid attention to. Her bank account was filling but her soul was emptying.

"I walked away from God and everything I knew to be right. I wasn't getting the results I wanted so I was going to take life into my own hands. And I did."

Heidi, despite her secretive life behind closed doors, was always there for her kids physically but emotionally and spiritually she was failing. Her sole purpose for exotic dancing was to be able to make enough money to escape the life she didn't want anymore. Her sole purpose, while with good intentions, came at the expense of her soul.

The easy road feels right for but a moment, but the difficult road will lead to the greatest reward. In the race of life, the pole position isn't always the best to be in.

With the love and affection she felt during work, albeit shallow and superficial, augmented her craving and desire for true intimate love and adoration. With a hardened heart, tired of dealing with drama, she met Scott. With only the intention of being friends, she fell for the way he made her feel, how he laughed with her and how he didn't cast any judgment. Friendship turned into companionship; companionship turned into an official relationship.

Scott and Heidi were both still officially married, although separated, and they each set court dates to divorce their spouses on the same day back to back in the same court room. They married a month later so they could officially wed before the baby they were having together would be born.

They had fallen in love but also fallen behind on bills.

Meanwhile, Scott and Heidi faced a devastating trial. At the time, Scott was a stenographer and tested the baby often. During the beginning of her second trimester, Heidi had a motherly intuition and a wanted to get the baby checked out to be safe. Performing an ultrasound, Scott couldn't find a heartbeat and they had to endure an emotionally devastating miscarriage.

Heidi went back to the strip club after losing the baby and worked a lot. She drowned out the pain by drinking and popping anxiety pills. It started to eat her up more and more every day.

Loss is a part of life. With it, we often gain so much more. Death is not the greatest loss in life; the greatest loss is what dies inside while still alive.

All things considered, we cannot wholly accept another's love for a second without first lavishly loving ourselves first.

"God felt so far away from me. I felt like demons were ripping me apart. I didn't feel like I could ever be normal again, accepted, respected or any kind of positive example. I even asked God to give me Cancer so I could die a slow death and then ask God for repentance. I thought in that process my kids would love me again. I didn't want to live anymore. Eventually I realized he wasn't distant, I was just so far away from Him."

In the end, there is no greater love than that of our Savior.

When we keep the faith, even when we cannot see past our demanding circumstances, we must trust that our hardest times often lead to the greatest moments. The best feeling in the world is watching things finally fall into place after watching them fall apart for so long.

When we keep driving forward, keeping the faith and let Jesus take the wheel, the road will lead us to salvation and reconciliation.

What does it profit to gain the world and lose our soul? God will never leave us or forsake us, for Heaven's sake.

"He never left me and never broke his covenant with me. I walked away but he never walked away from me. He stayed by my side even in the really disgusting times in my life. He loved me anyways."

It was so hard and scary to leave her biggest source of income but she remembered God's word when he said he will never leave us or forsake us. After 6 years working in the strip club industry Heidi finally made the decision to leave that lifestyle for good. She knew her marriage to Scott would be very rocky and he wouldn't be happy with my choice because it would be a huge loss of income. She told God that even if Scott left her, she will serve him anyways.

Scott was baptized a few months later and together they walk in truth and unbounding faith.

Her relationship with her children continues to get stronger.

Through her journey from darkness to light, she has shined bright for others to walk the righteous path.

Heidi getting lost essentially allowed others to be saved.

Heidi shifted gears and went in a new direction. She threw away her old life in hopes of restoration and a renewed spirit. She devoted herself to His calling for her life.

Heidi started attending real estate school and quickly became one of the top producing real estate agents. She went from broken homes to selling houses. She found peace with her own body, a temple designed to be used to serve others not be used and abused by others.

Real estate helped her be surrounded by real people and produce real sustainability. Due to her unparalleled growth and success, she has been rewarded with the privilege of teaching success school to other realtors.

Being a true follower of Christ is allowing her to lead others.

"I'm continuing to be the best that I can be. I know that through all this, through all the pain and brokenness, I was never forgotten. I was worth it. No matter how horrible and ugly you feel, there is always redemption. There is always a way out. There is always grace and forgiveness. There is always love."

The community we associate ourselves with determines our direction and speed: being around positive people who encourage you, serves as the vehicle to improved self-worth and self-confidence.

So many people want to fit in when we were born to stand out. We are all worthy and we all belong. Surround yourself only with people who will lift you higher. We can change the people around us and we can change the people we choose to be around. Ultimately, we shouldn't be conformed by the patterns of the world but become transformed by the renewing of our minds and souls.

Compassion is the key to a fulfilled life. Everyone is worth it. When you believe how much you're worth, you'll stop discounting all your shortcomings. Our value doesn't decrease based on other's inability to see our worth. Sometimes the hardest part of the journey is believing you're worthy of the trip.

Shifting gears is the start to a new life, one paved with hopes and dreams, purpose and passion. Redirecting your mind will redirect your life. "I envision where I'm supposed to be and it drives me. I have some fears that attempt to hold me back but I use them as fuel to push me to the next level."

You cannot break records with your foot on the brake.

We only have one life to make the best life.

"God has given me so much so how can I not give so much back to him?" He has given me so many gifts and I can't stand to not use them for His glory. That's what ultimately drives me," Heidi authorizes.

Stay positive and when life is negative, shift gears at least remain grateful. People's opinion of you does not need to be your reality. Nobody can define your worth unless you let them. When you are going through Hell, sprint. Heaven is just beyond the next turn and God will always bless the broken road.

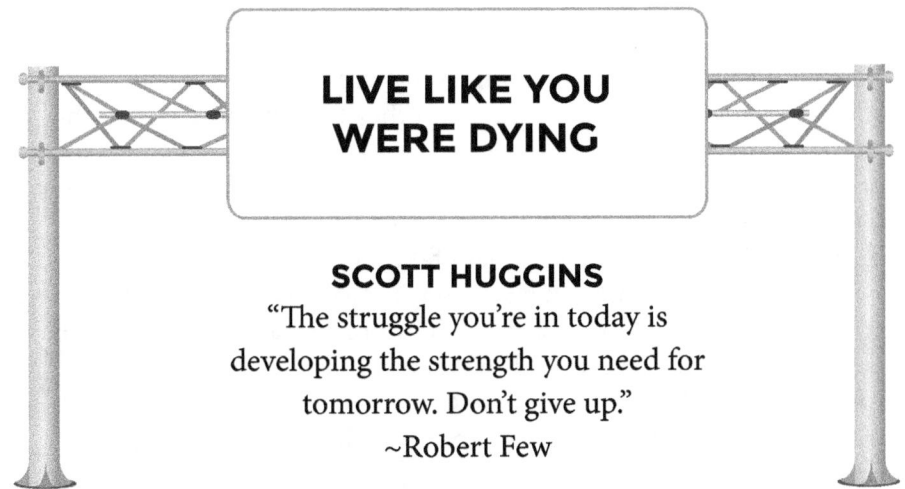

LIVE LIKE YOU WERE DYING

SCOTT HUGGINS

"The struggle you're in today is developing the strength you need for tomorrow. Don't give up."
~Robert Few

Obstacles early in life elevate you to the next level later on. Surrounding ourselves with those who help us rise when life crashes in on us, serves as the catalyst to uplift our spirits in times of adversity. Sometimes life is about risking everything for a dream no one can see but you.

At a young age, Scott Huggins' parents separated and his mother disappeared out of his life. His step mom's family owned a tobacco farm and he grew up learning the true meaning of a hard day's work. Working all summer, as tough as it was, Scott earned roughly $1000 that he used to buy school clothes and provide for his wants and needs.

Small town USA served as the vehicle for his BIG dreams. Our environment shapes who we become and while Scott lived on the outskirts of town, all of his childhood experiences helped him eventually create a life on the outskirts of heaven.

Eventually, Scott started working for his dad's company doing HVAC as well as mechanical contracting, and additionally a landscaping and handyman business on the side part time during the summers. He rarely ever got to slow down and discovered when you sit around idle you will get passed or run over. His desire to create a new life burned hot, and he hasn't cooled down since he started his first business in elementary school selling fake cigarettes, using envelopes as the cigarette wrapper and pencil shavings as the tobacco. Creatively and resourcefully, he filled discarded real Marlboro cigarette cases to make them look legitimate! He would sell them to his classmates and his business was smokin' hot! Ultimately, the staff stomped out his business and while he was the butt of jokes, he caught fire as an entrepreneur.

Scott made a decision that he was going to become someone different in order to get unparalleled results. He started making friends with all different cliques in order to show his peers his true character and that a physical restriction is not a full limitation. Yet, with an understanding that others see us through their eyes, and they were looking at him differently because of his lazy eye, Scott wanted to get it fixed. He begged his dad and his stepmom but was denied. He ultimately convinced his grandparents to pay for the surgery. With his first big sale, he caught the image of creating a new life for himself. He realized sight is not nearly as important as vision.

Although he had a lazy eye, Scott was never indolent as a worker and kept his eye on the prize.

During his transition into high school, Scott knew he wanted to do something dissimilar because he was different. "I was thinking bigger than the small town and the circumstances I was in. I didn't know where it was going to go or what direction. But I knew this was my time to shine and time to change things," Scott proclaimed.

When our circumstances create a life that is less than desirable, shifting gears and pursuing our hopes and dreams leads to the right lane!

"I would take any opportunity to get out of my comfort zone and put myself out there," he professes. "I knew I was going to do something besides stay where I was and I knew I was going to go do something greater."

Scott joined every club he could and helped found the first swimming team at their high school. From playing football to learning Latin and dramatic interpretation through the Latin Club, Scott leveraged every chance to make a change. "I just said yes and figured it out as I went." That led to Scott traveling the entire country performing and winning awards, getting a taste for life outside his small home town. At the time, Scott was nominated for Boys State and made it to the first national level competition and also had the honor of meeting Senator Strom Thurmond. More important than the accolades was the self-confidence he achieved.

Then life changed and Scott was forced to rely on his journey to protect his family and his future.

One day playing with his personal electronic kit, tapping into their home phone, he unexpectedly overheard his stepmom talking to a man in the way she should only talk to her husband. Scott really struggled how to handle the reality before him.

This was a huge burden.

Scott spent several days agonizing over what to do and how to approach it or if he should even say anything at all. When what he thought was a good opportunity, he brought it up to his dad while we working on a job together. Much to Scott's amazement and refreshing relief of his dad's knowledge of the affair, Scott was empathetic, yet challenged at the same time. He knew his life was going to change because of the inevitable direction it would go when they faced the truth behind the infidelity.

He moved in with his grandparents and while the new situation was unique, he didn't realize how much his life would really change for a reason far worse than the immorality in his home.

May 31, 1992, about one week prior to high school graduation, attending a pre-graduation ceremony to receive an award, Scott's life would change forever. Around midnight, his grandmother entered his bedroom sobbing uncontrollably which was astonishing and unnerving because Scott had never heard his grandma cry before. His grandmother proceeded to inform Scott that his father had been shot and killed. "I just remember feeling like it was a dream," but unfortunately it was actually a nightmare no child should ever endure.

While ruminating on the news, Scott never imagined it would go from bad to worse.

He soon discovered his step mom was involved.

After they left the graduation ceremony, they went out on the town and had some drinks. His stepmom had put a sedative into his dad's drink, incapacitating him, essentially rendering him comatose. She drove him to the man's house with whom she was having an affair. He was a state trooper, and armed, he shot Scott's dad in the head point blank.

Despite the emotional overload and devastating reality of infidelity, Scott's dad was hoping to keep their family together.

Instead, what happened that night tore Scott's world apart.

Despite the anguish, Scott went on to attend the College of Charleston in August of 1992 and Charleston became home. While he was in college his stepmom and his father's killer were both convicted in March 1994 and sentenced to 25 years in prison. Even though they were found guilty, Scott's heart was still convicted. He thought it was the end of the road, but there were still many truths to uncover.

Scott graduated in 1996 with a BS in Biology and minor in Chemistry.

In January 1997, both his stepmom and his dad's killer were released on a technicality and were facing a retrial. When the attorneys went to prepare for the retrial Scott found out most of the evidence had disappeared from the police evidence room. Both ended up pleading guilty in September 1997 and getting time served to avoid another trial. Scott did not discover until 14 years after graduating college in 2010 that his dad's killer had relocated 10 minutes away from him when he discovered he had opened a business in the area. How is it possible that out of the entire state, let alone the entire country, he ended up settling just down the road from Scott? Almost every day he drove by his business and it was a constant reminder of the calamity he bestowed upon Scott's dad and his family.

God was truly testing Scott.

When life takes a wrong turn, how we handle it determines our next direction.

Do you turn left when nothing is right or turn right when you have nothing left?

The biggest shift Scott had to face was determining what drives him to truly live.

"I had to learn to live and let that go," Scott attributes to his devout faith in God. "One of the hardest things to do in life is to forgive somebody. When I first got saved, I was listening to a sermon about how Jesus forgave the Roman soldier who persecuted him. So who was I to not forgive the people in my life for what wrongs they have done us?" Scott professes. "I had to forgive them more for myself so I could move on with my own life."

The heaviest thing we can hold in life is a grudge.

The biggest Lane Change anyone could possibly face is to have both your parents taken away in an instant. Scott had to face himself and his new reality. He made a decision that anything he was going to do and whoever he was going to become was up to him.

If you're going to make it happen when your world gets turned upside down, it's up to you.

Scott committed to staying true to his goal of attending college. He barely squeezed by because he started partying to escape some of his reality.

Some people are on the right track going the wrong way. Others are on the wrong track going the right way.

Scott got his act together and got on the right track going the right way.

While pursuing medical school, he got surgical with his studies but because of his grades, starting his college career, he struggled to pass the exam and qualify for medical school.

Meanwhile, his friend had introduced him to the company Amway and he joined in hopes of making a fortune. In the grand scheme of things, he didn't strike it rich but he became extremely wealthy as a person. Thanks to Amway, Scott got his first exposure to personal development and a crash course in sales. One of the books he was given during that time was "Think and Grow Rich" by Napoleon Hill. It made huge impact on him and challenged his way of thinking. "I'm very thankful for that experience because one of the most life-changing things you can do is improve yourself by reading and learning as much as you can. Most people think after you're done with school, you're done, but that's really when it all begins."

Scott discovered how difficult sales can be and how challenging managing people can be. He truly understood that in school we are taught lessons and then given tests, where as in the business world we are given tests and we determine the lesson.

While he didn't make his millions, the experience and person he became was priceless.

More importantly, when we take action and move forward in life, even when it feels like we are at a dead end, shifting gears and driving forward is the key to progress.

Scott's same friend who enrolled him in Amway, a never-ceasing entrepreneur, found a new opportunity learning how to buy foreclosure properties. The two of them, along with one other friend, pooled all their money together and with $500, approached the gentlemen on the late-night infomercial ready to purchase his program. When they found out it was $2500, they were immediately deflated, but they were graciously accepted into the program for $500. They would later find out the man was convicted for bank and wire fraud and imprisoned. While that gentleman was jailed, this program was legitimate and set Scott toward a life of freedom and autonomy.

But there is always a cost.

"When you're talking to people who don't dream big and have the same vision you do, they try to discourage you. Thank goodness I didn't listen to them," Scott declares. "I just kept educating myself and learning everything I could to avoid the problems those people were talking about."

When you don't know where you're going, any road will take you there. When you know your destination, you can avoid the roadblocks and handle the detours easier because you're a more skilled driver!

Scott remained persistent and consistent despite the hard work and time-consuming effort. Just because he was a broke college student didn't mean he had to have his aspirations crash on the boulevard of broken dreams.

When life forecloses on you, keep offering your best!

When you offer your best, you'll attract even greater things!!

Investing in yourself pays the highest ROI and investing in your craft will pay dividends forever.

Shifting Gears

The first deal Scott closed in downtown Charleston for roughly $12,000 was an area you wouldn't want to be alone in at night. He borrowed the funds from his grandfather. He still owns that property today and it's worth nearly $300,000! Venture to say, his diligence and hard work paid off and continues to pay him today! He was able to turn that first borrowed $12k investment into a small portfolio worth $1.3 million.

Scott had fallen in love with real estate and shortly after fell in love with the woman who would become his first wife.

His dreams grew along with his knowledge of the industry. He quickly discovered that in order to purchase more properties, the banks wanted to see a consistent and steady income. Often in order to get to the next level we must do whatever necessary to advance; and, it's those who do what others won't that achieve what those others never will.

Scott had experience doing due diligence on foreclosure and now it was time to do due diligence on the best road that would take him to his desired destination. He discovered that ultrasound would be the degree he could achieve with the least amount of time and greatest return. Real estate was his new baby but it was ultrasound that would help birth his biggest accomplishments!

Scott was earning nearly $200,000 gross a year between his salary working as a contractor traveling from hospital to hospital along with his more passive rental income. He swiftly realized that paychecks do not get you as far as you think. While most become complacent with steady income, he was leveraging the income to earn even more. Sometimes our greatest asset is our determination and will to succeed.

He didn't want to wait to buy real estate; Scott wanted to buy real estate and wait.

Scott grew his portfolio impressively but then hit a wall as residential lenders limit the number of home loans you can have. He hit a standstill, but realized he couldn't stand still and consequently rerouted to continue driving forward.

His wife wanted to go back to school so he took a job at the Medical University of South Carolina. Since she had supported him he felt the need to return the support. Each house needs a good support system and every entrepreneur needs the same thing. Ten years later at that same job, Scott ended up on a road that he hadn't planned to take for that long. "One day you wake up and realize this wasn't my plan. I made a mistake. I got comfortable. I got used to having that steady income and having benefits and the 'security blanket.' I got distracted and it took my focus of what my real goal was. I hope a lot of people wake up before I do."

When we replace our hopes and dreams with comfort and complacency, we eventually become replaced by someone who remains focused on their ultimate road to greatness.

With a focused attention on the distractions in life, Scott and his wife began drifting apart.

Scott discovered the importance of mentorship. His wife's brother started teaching him the importance of being physically fit and the correlation to being fiscally fit. As they created a more intimate relationship, their bond grew with Scott's passion for fitness.

He discovered that all the money in the world doesn't matter if you can't enjoy it. Moreover, sometimes the pursuit of our dreams that make us come alive can actually become the death of us.

One night with a knock on the door, Scott opened it to greet a coroner who shared that his mentor, friend and brother-in-law had died from a complication with some drugs, creating life-ending heart failure. Scott, doing the hardest thing he ever had to do, called his in laws to share the news.

A few years later, Scott filed for a divorce.

While separation is never easy, it was even harder because economically the United States was in the great recession and property values had decreased considerably. They had to divide their assets and Scott's credit took a major hit, too.

One speed bump after another.

Never short sale a winner, though!

Thankfully, Scott had bought his properties the right way and was able to bide his time slightly.

At the same time, Scott met his now wife, Heidi, who was going through a divorce and providing for 5 sons. They were both starting over but never underestimated their potential together.

The hardest part of beginning again, is beginning. In the end, though, when you do it the right way it makes it all worth it.

They fell in love but fell back into unhealthy habits that distracted them from their purpose. They blew through a lot of money when they should have been investing that money back into building their real estate empire.

All the years of doing something the wrong way can be changed rapidly with the help of someone who can show you how to do it the right way. Heidi made a commitment to quit her job that was hurting their future in exchange for taking the necessary steps to create their future.

Changing a few things and shifting gears slightly can change your entire life.

"If she hadn't made that decision we wouldn't be where we are today. I would have been going down the same road," Scott admits.

With the burden on his shoulders to solely provide financially, Scott selfishly blamed her for actually doing what was the best thing for their family. Heidi was intentionally rekindling her relationship with God which ignited a fire for both of them to fuel their vision. Often, we look inwardly, when outwardly we cannot see the gifts and blessings that God has for us if we are open to the opportunity for those sanctifications.

Scott and Heidi created a road map and game plan for the next chapter of their lives. While Heidi wanted to go back to the radiology field, Scott challenged her to consider real estate. With a passion for it, Heidi agreed and went to real estate school to get her license. They both wanted to get closer to a Heavenly relationship but they were both working ungodly hours.

They continue to pray together, stay together and slay together! They became an unstoppable power couple leveraging each other's gifts and talents along with a family life balance to create a divine lifestyle.

Scott had set out in the real estate industry to make a lot of money and create massive wealth. Scott started investing in himself again, realizing the only permanent thing in life is change.

When he got baptized and committed his life to the Great Commission, it was their commissions that became the blessings for other people. He discovered the truth of why he was put on this avenue in life. "I started thinking bigger. I want to change the world and have an impact on people and change their lives. It dawned on me to give more. We give to change other people's lives but also to change our own heart. It has fundamentally changed who I am at my core."

Scott grew to know his Heavenly father which begged the question who his biological mother was. On a quest to locate her, he found her close to his childhood home town, barely scraping by and dependent on government subsidies. While upset with her and confused by the demons she was experiencing, he realized that if she had been in the picture his whole life, perhaps it would have taken a different course.

Scott had the desire to help, yet because they had just rekindled the relationship he didn't truly know how to help her or how bad it really was for her.

Shortly after reconnecting with his biological mother, he got another proverbial knock on the door. This time, it was a phone call to let him know his mother had committed suicide by overdosing on prescription medication. 6 months after she came into his life she was gone again just like that. It was a roll coaster of emotions. The ups and downs created a myriad of sentiments – guilt that he did not do enough and anger that she did that to him again.

With all the loss and deaths in his life, Scott had to die to himself and his faith to truly live.

Scott's had many calls and knocks that changed his life.

In our own lives, ultimately, it's our call to shift gears for ourselves and those we are called to impact. When we ask, seek and knock, the doors will open to blessings beyond our wildest imagination.

A lot of people in our lives distract us from our goals and dreams. They attempt to bring us down when we are working to escalate our success. They believe they are doing it to protect us; yet, it's our tenacity, self-improvement and steadfast faith that will protect us among life's tests.

"You're in control of your life, no one else is. Make a decision and take action. Get out of your comfort zone and do it. The difference between a successful person who will achieve their dreams and those who won't is how well you roll with the punches. They're either going to build you up or tear you down."

Failure and loss are ultimately life's greatest teachers.

Transitions are never ending. While we can prepare for life's twists and turns, it is our ability to courageously adapt and shift gears when they happen that equip us the greatest to change the world.

God loves you infinitely and wants you in His presence every moment, and if He knows that Heaven is a much better place for you, then why on Earth has he left you here?

That is where the rubber meets the road. Let Jesus take the wheel and drive on!

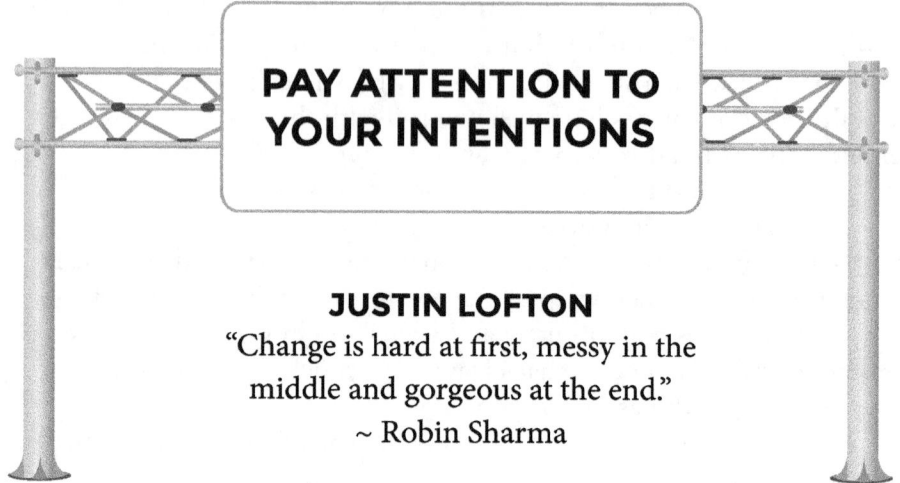

JUSTIN LOFTON
"Change is hard at first, messy in the middle and gorgeous at the end."
~ Robin Sharma

We go through life with an apparent reality based on the journey each of us has traveled. As we drive forward, focusing on the road ahead, looking in the rearview mirror only long enough to reflect on where we have been, the person we see in the reflection may be someone totally different than we perceive ourselves to be. Your own eyes gazing back at you, observing your surroundings through your peripheral while gripping the steering wheel; as you reflect on the times you have had to grip on to life just to hold on, you recognize your life's destination is a result of the roads you have been down before.

Some people come into our lives to help us realize that we deserve better and there are others who help us realize that better is what we already have. Justin Lofton is a leader who brings out the best in others because he has had to bring out the best in himself.

At a very early age, his parents divorced. Justin found himself taking things apart during his childhood, potentially because he felt his world had been torn apart at one point. Throughout his life, he has always been inquisitive, assessing how things work and why they operate a certain way. Ultimately, this forced him to figure out his place in the world and how he fits in the framework of society.

Justin started his first business at age eight, fixing and repairing bicycles for other kids in the neighborhood. The venture only lasted two weeks because he listened to the advice of the older kids who told him how foolish he was and that it would never work. With a young and vulnerable self-esteem (not the confident man he is today), Justin allowed the opinions of him and his potential, or lack thereof, to become his reality. While he enjoyed doing the repairs and wanted to help others, like many of us, he allowed others to determine his path.

Justin had a solid core group of friends and Jeff and Mark Winking became two of his best friends. Because he was raised by his mother and sister, Jeff and Mark essentially became Justin's brothers and extended family. Vastly different because their parents were financially successful, unlike his mother who carried two jobs just to provide for Justin and his sister, the Winking family taught Justin priceless life lessons. Their father who was in the technology world and owned a personal computer, before the Internet was mainstream, connected to Prodigy, and in essence, connected Justin to a whole new world. This became a pivotal lane change for Justin because it exposed him to a novel dimension; and Mr. Winking's expertise of the technology connected him to the power of a whole new world.

Shortly after falling in love with the idea of a virtual world, Justin saw a video camera at a yard sale across the street from his house. It was a giant box where you inserted a VHS tape with a big wire that connected it to a 50-pound camera you had to carry on your shoulder. With a price tag of $300, Justin simply couldn't shoulder the burden of the expense because he didn't have the resources. But he absolutely had the resourcefulness.

"When I figure out what I want, I figure out how to get it," Justin boldly confirms.

He asked his mom for the money and when he was denied, he became creative. Justin started a landscaping business going door to door to promote his services. While it earned him some cash, he quickly learned that businesses with seasonality create cash-flow challenges. "I had a business mind even as a kid," he acknowledges. "I was always thinking about what I could do."

While he was always working on fattening his pockets, his weight became an issue and Justin became fat himself. Without a father figure in his life, when his emotions became overwhelming, he turned to food for validation. In a small suburb outside Atlanta, a new McDonald's opened when Justin was 14 and he got a job working as a cash register. While he wasn't allowed to work in the kitchen, his inquisitions lead him to learn all aspects of the business. Within a couple years, Justin was managing the restaurant, exposing him to the systems, automation and scalability of a business. "I saw how processes helped young people operate a business very efficiently to provide value to the marketplace that was consistent."

Flipping burgers flipped Justin's paradigm about business. While the food was terrible for you, Justin ate up all the knowledge he could and started to taste!

When Justin was entering his later years of high school, his mother had to relocate to another town and Justin started living on his own for the first time. He discovered a passion for fitness and sports nutrition and shifted gears from being in the slow lane to the fast lane by accelerating his path to optimal health. "It was a key lane change for me. It shifted how I lived my life and it became a lifestyle change. It falls back to my desire to take things apart and put them back together and I began doing that with the human body." His passion lead him to study sports nutrition at Kennesaw State University. While his body was burning fat, he was burning the midnight oil with his newest business, Shaded Perspectives, a car window tinting business. He recognized that studying the human body was more of a hobby because he didn't see a lucrative path, and his entrepreneurial spirit drove him out of college and into the business lane.

"I felt like I needed to get out the bubble I grew up in to really expand my horizons and figure out what I wanted to do for myself long term." Justin moved to New York City to live with his sister and barely made ends meet as a personal trainer. Essentially an adult babysitter for his clients, he was leveraging his passion for fitness; yet, counterproductively because he invested so much time into the health of his clients, his own health began to diminish. "The move to a new city was a huge lane change because it helped me see the world in a different light, to see a diverse perspective and see life move at a much faster pace."

As our perspective shifts, so does life and the direction we go. Justin's sister fell in love with a guy and they were moving to California. When they offered Justin to go with them, he accepted and began working for their family company as a plumber. He realized through the experience of making good money and fixing things, that he was still limited to trading time for dollars. Plumbing provided him the realization that it was time to stop working with his hands and start working with his head. He was tired of dealing with crap and didn't want wealth to remain a pipe dream!!

Like always, when he had a vision for what he wanted, Justin acted immediately to shift and develop the skills and intellect he needed to succeed in a new industry. He began studying information technology. He started working for a small integration company while selling nutritional supplements online to supplement his income. Before the Internet, he had to drive his sales using overture to drive traffic to his stores. He built successful online stores that created massive results, which built his confidence in the digital world. While working at the IT company he saw numerous opportunities as an IT engineer through his entrepreneurial lenses. Justin recognized the shift in retail sales to service-based products so he launched a refurbished equipment division and began managing a team of IT engineers.

When you see a shift in the market, perhaps that's the best time to shift gears and get into the lane where the traffic will flow to you.

With a newfound passion and the success to support it, Justin began consulting companies to facilitate their expansion and implementation of online development, marketing and sales for their businesses. He was able to help double and triple the revenue for some companies in less than 24 months. One of those businesses happened to be his dad's company. While his father wasn't present in Justin's life as a dad, one of the best presents Justin could give to his dad was accelerated growth for his company. "Supporting my dad was a way to rekindle our relationship. We were both entrepreneurial minded and he had a successful business that was starting to slip, and I was having great success with marketing online. It became a way to fuel success together."

Helping these few companies burned a new passion and rekindled Justin's desire to help more people. All the lanes Justin had traveled merged into an intersection of his skills, passions and drive to create success. Justin's focus shift from making money to making a difference and his true fulfillment came from helping others.

Justin launched his most successful business, FreshAgency, because he wanted to be able to diversify his knowledge and time to exponentially help as many companies and people as possible. His agency, a full-service digital marketing firm, exploded and catapulted his success into the fast lane.

With increased exposure to the high life, Justin discovered that business prosperity is fulfilling, but familial richness was indescribable. While he was supporting his father's business, he became a father himself when his daughter, Amaya, was born. Within a year of entering the world, she was diagnosed with Autism. "Being faced with the challenge of helping my beautiful daughter overcome that and support her, as well as starting the agency, emotionally and financially, was truly a lane change. I saw life in a different light again supporting someone who couldn't support herself. More so, being fully independent and having that added responsibility, truly shifted my focus from making money to delivering value."

While nurturing Amaya, he was nurturing all his new businesses in their infancy, too.

Continuing to see gaps in the market, along with the desire to provide for his family, Justin launched a new company, SyncSumo, the leading online advertising software program to integrate Facebook ads with custom audience syncing solution. The development of this leading concept afforded Justin the ability to expand globally, fulfilling his yearning to help more people. Justin's ability to create dynamic leverage has afforded him the capacity to capitalize personally and financially, while supporting entrepreneurs and businesses through his various platforms.

"At the core of it, you must be able to look in the mirror, and love who you see. It's not an easy task. We all judge ourselves on what's imaginable for us and the key is to accept yourself for who you are right in this moment. That's when the doors of opportunity and possibilities open for you. We look around and compare ourselves to the people we hang out with; it's about tuning out those distractions and finding your core value in this world and work hard every day to tap into the power you possess to deliver that unique value."

Finding your natural flow is paramount. If you are pushing against that flow, attempting to surpass it, you're doing yourself and those you want to serve a disservice. Patience and persistence is pivotal on the road to success. The process is the journey. Direction is important but sometimes it's taking the next step in any direction which may lead to the shift you need to succeed. When you find your flow and direction, move as fast as you can. Directional shifts will direct your path. Change is inevitable. Every day is a new day but we will have changed from the previous day as will the world. Our role is to adapt, shift gears and accelerate our desires.

When you put focused attention on the key intentions, you will start the vehicle that drives your life and business forward.

There is no shortage of money; only a shortage of people really going for it. Sometimes the road to success seems never ending but it's the glimpse of what's to come that keeps us motivated. The thing about motivated people chasing their dreams is they look crazy to lazy people. Trust that when the answer is no, it may just mean it's time to shift gears because there is certainly a better yes down the road. When you can't stop thinking about it, don't stop working for it – all you need is the plan, the roadmap and courage to press on to your destination.

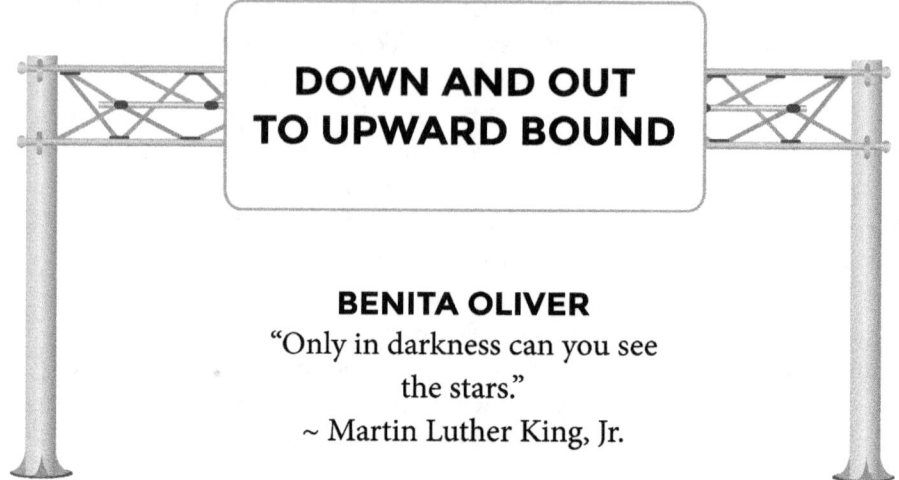

BENITA OLIVER

"Only in darkness can you see the stars."
~ Martin Luther King, Jr.

Often it is the moments in life where we are forced to make split decisions that define our next course of action.

Benita Oliver's life completely shifted gears when she was 3 years old after her parents divorced, and she was uprooted from the home she grew up in and moved in with her grandmother. Raised by a single mother in a new and unfamiliar environment, dividing her time between Ohio during the school year and Michigan with her father for the summers, Benita had a new set of rules and a new set of circumstances that created an entirely new reality. As a result of her parents splitting, she was forced to split time accordingly.

"I had to come to the realization of what it was like to not really choose an outcome, figure everything out and figure out why it happened," Benita recalls. Her unsuccessful attempts to get her parents back together because of her desire for a healthy family life forced her to accept the truth. Yet, she did not settle for an involuntary reality. With a forced independence and the need to find her own way, God's unrelenting voice encouraged and motivated the desire for more for her life. She relied on her strength when weakness could have conquered her. Despite the unfortunate situation, Benita was still able to acknowledge that she still had both her parents. During that trivial time, she was capable of looking at the bright side of a dark situation. "It's up to you in life who you become, who you want to be, and it doesn't matter who's there or not. You are living your life for you."

Every child yearns for love and affection from her parents. Benita began exceeding in school with the earnest commitment to herself and the desire to impress her parents. She commanded a lot from herself and became very active in numerous activities, pursuing greatness and success in all she chased. "Throughout life I continued to accomplish things for myself to make myself feel good and to set myself up for the next chapter." Many stay stuck in the same season because of the limits they create based on somebody else's expectations. You cannot start a new chapter of your life if you keep re-reading the last one. The key is to learn from that chapter and re-write your own story. Like a book, every day is a new page; every month is a new chapter, every year is a new series.

Through the Upward Bound program, an organization that provides opportunities for participants to succeed in their precollege pursuits, Benita discovered a deeper sense of self-worth. With an emphasis on education, she realized that she had to push herself in every aspect of her life knowing the way we do one thing, is the way we do everything. She understood the idea that birds of a feather flock together and she began surrounding herself with good people and successful leaders to soar to new heights. "I knew I wanted something different for my life and I knew it had to start with me doing the right things." Ultimately, if we want to go the right way we have to let go of the wrong people and the wrong habits that would lead us down the wrong avenues.

Benita found herself among a group of friends who had another crowd of friends they didn't want her to be associated with. Stuck in the middle, she ended up in a fight that got her suspended from school. While Benita wasn't the instigator and was mostly the object of other's behaviors, she became responsible for the outcome. "It really made me look at things differently as far as the negative things in life that come at you. It gave me a different approach on things."

Teenage years for most females bring with them many daily trials and tribulations, challenges that change them dramatically, partly because of all the drama. For many, drama pervades their entire life because they thrive on their own insecurities. The more we allow it in our lives the greater the level of frustration and the seemingly endless struggle to escape their own creation. Losers play victim to the circumstances they created. People who have no life will always try to start drama in yours. There comes a time when you have to let go of all the pointless pettiness and the people who create it to allow yourself space to allow people who encourage you and make you so happy you forget the bad and focus solely on the good.

Benita got involved in a mediation program to educate others about conflict resolution. Our ability to manage our environment and our emotions determines our results. Life is full of challenges and our ability to solve problems is essential to our growth and maturity. If you want to escalate your position in life, you have to learn how to de-escalate negativity. If you want to own an abundant life, you must take ownership of yours. Sometimes that means fighting back for what you believe and other times it means walking away to put yourself in a healthier position to fight even harder for what you want. When life pushes on you, push back. When others push back on you, let them stumble over their own triviality.

Expect difficulties and moments in life that force you to dig deep.

A few years later, Benita went away to college at The University of Toledo and faced a bigger hardship. She lost her grandmother the day after she arrived home for winter break. Benita was hurt, angry and frustrated, because her family hadn't told her of her grandmother's condition. She felt like if she had known, she could have come home sooner. "Time is something you can never get back."

These life-changing moments force us to catch our own breath.

Heartbroken, Benita lost one of the most important influences in her life. She also realized the house she would have gone home to for the summer was going to be sold and she wouldn't have anywhere to stay, that felt like home.

Where do you turn when you're forced to shift gears?

Sometimes we have to go backward to move forward. Other times we have to stop moving forward and reflect on what got us to the place we are. Benita was living out of suitcase, essentially homeless. "I saw everything in a different light and I needed to grow up even more," Benita recalls. "Once you have tasted independence, you want more of it." She went back to school, began working three jobs to afford an apartment to live on her own and start creating a new reality for herself. "I've always had that mentality that no matter what I go through, what doesn't kill me makes me stronger. I'm going to survive and move on to the next phase."

Like a track hurdler, it becomes necessary to allow space to jump over the hurdle because of the momentum that was created. In life and business, you cannot go back in time to make a new start but you can go forward in time and make a new ending by what you do better today. Mentorship provides the ability for their hindsight to serve as our foresight. We can all learn from problems and often, it's better to learn from someone else's. Success leaves clues and successful people can clue you into what helped them accomplish great things.

Benita had the drive to create a better life. She decided becoming a physician assistant would afford her the ability to pursue her dreams. "I wanted a change of scenery and a change of environment. I needed a change of everything!" She decided to attend the University of Colorado Denver Health and Science Center and stay with her family who had always supported her, unconditionally. Her aunt was getting her a job with her doctor and that would help put her back on track going the right way. She was living at Mile High while her dreams remained sky high!

Her newfound success caused her to start thinking differently and approaching life in a unique way. She started challenging herself and questioning the possibilities she could accomplish. When we start to open ourselves to new possibilities, renewed opportunities come our way.

Benita's openness led her to the morning newspaper that spoke to hear in black and white. It wasn't the articles or headlines that grabbed her attention, but an ad that she saw that read "Must love Money, Music and Fun!" It was music to hear heart and soul and she desired to have fun while earning more! It was as if her desire to succeed and her willingness to advance herself were in perfect harmony.

The opportunity was a sales position with a fragrance company. The career change had a sweet smell to it and an even more perfumed potential. Between the interim of starting her residency and working for the doctor, opportunity was right under her nose and the financial reward was nothing to sneeze at! Often in life, divine opportunities present themselves and we overlook the gift of happenstance when at the heart level we know it's an unknown possibility disguised as blessing. Benita seized the opportunity immediately and never looked back.

With massive success early in her new endeavor, Benita relocated to North Carolina to open her own fragrance company. The aroma of victory never smelled so good!

Celebrating their success as a company, Benita's took her top 5 salespersons to visit Washington, DC to enjoy the historic inauguration of President Obama and to celebrate their monumental performances.

When they returned home, Benita returned to an office filled with water from a burst pipe and not only was the office submerged, but she was flooded with overwhelming emotions. When everything you have built as a leader is under water, you must respond positively and help your team rise up with you.

When life shifts, you have to move accordingly.

"It's not how hard you fall it's how quick you get back up," Benita proclaims. "There is always something you can do in your circumstances. There is nothing you can't accomplish or get through."

When stuff in your life breaks down, don't let it break you.

Turmoil creates an opportunity to create a turn around.

Benita turned her focus to her team and their wishes in time of need.

"When you're running a business, it's not just about you but the people around you. The speed of the leader determines the speed of the pack. Your team is only going to go off of what you do and how you respond to adversities."

With leadership comes great responsibility.

When you find your lane, own it and drive the world forward paving the way for others to follow.

"Once I got into my field, I worked like a horse with blinders on. I didn't look to the left or right, I just focused on my goals ahead. Even when things are going great you have to prepare yourself for the future."

Benita prides herself on the relationship focus in her sales and marketing. She doesn't look at people as a sale, but rather at each sale as a new relationship. She believes a satisfied customer is the best business strategy of all. Ultimately, sales go up and down but service stays forever. Build rapport and your business will grow faster.

There have been significant moments that have altered the direction your life has gone. Each of the decisions you've made has created the reality you're experiencing today. Many of those instances were in your control and many of them were out of your control.

These significant moments have affected your beliefs, your paradigms, your perception of the world around you and even, unbeknownst to you, the actions you have taken as a result. The significance of those moments was unconsciously determined by you and can be seen outwardly by the way you're living your life every day.

Moment by moment your thoughts have become the patterns that appear in your life and those patterns have created your daily actions.

Your actions have led to the results you have right now.

Do not let life bully you. Learn to fight back when compulsory and walk away when relevant.

Reflect on the moments that have forever changed the direction of your life, both the moments where in an instant you knew your life would never be the same, as well as the moments where you didn't know why they happened until you looked back and hindsight cued you in on the exact reason.

"It doesn't matter what you went to school for. Follow your dreams and what you aspire to do. Find what you're good at and be great at it!" Benita implores.

Benita is currently on a new journey helping Urban Barber College in San Diego market their school as the best barber college to attend in California.

It is definitely a cut above the rest!

Blind-faith moves may lead you to a renewed vision for your life. Along the lanes you travel, when you do so with resolute trust and solemn passion, you'll learn the way, pave the way and lead the way for others on every journey you pursue.

When you shift gears, take massive action even despite unfavorable circumstances and remain persistent in your drive for greatness. Consequently, your life will become a model for others to go from being down and out to upward bound!

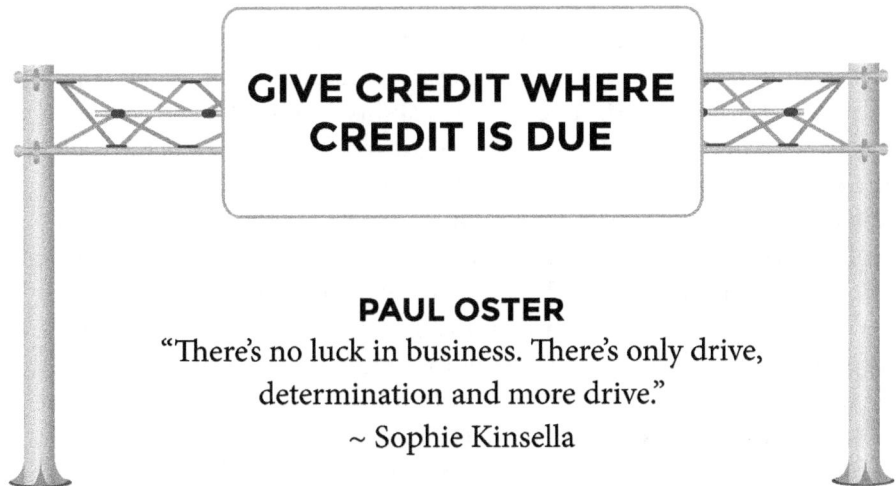

GIVE CREDIT WHERE CREDIT IS DUE

PAUL OSTER

"There's no luck in business. There's only drive, determination and more drive."
~ Sophie Kinsella

We experience life's moments and habitually don't understand the value of them until they become memories. Through childhood, these moments shape who we are and the direction of our early years. Those things out of our control become what we want to control later in life; if we aren't where we want, we must shift and reroute or we could end up on the boulevard of broken dreams.

Paul Oster has become successful personally and professionally and attributes much of it to the work ethic he developed because of his parent's separation, thus being forced to take on responsibility early in life. Raised by a single parent on welfare, he believes it was a blessing in disguise because it taught him lessons he may not have learned otherwise. More, often people get upset with the results they don't get from the work they don't do. Ultimately, all roads that lead to success must pass through hard work boulevard at some point. Often people talk about the value of the dollar more than the value of working toward that dollar.

The division between Paul's family and others was a highway that separated the lower socioeconomic families and those with more affluence. Through middle school, his ability to interact with everyone helped him discover it didn't matter how many assets you had or where you were from, instead it had everything to do with your drive and motivation to get where you wanted. A burning desire was fueled in Paul to fervently accomplish all that he wanted because success was an open road that anyone can drive. Most just exit before they even start.

Success occurs when your dreams become bigger than your excuses. Paul's drive and determination, on his own dime, afforded him the opportunity to be the first of his family to attend college. While it took him seven years, he graduated with a BS in Health and Physical Education and recognized that you may not arrive as fast as others but if you're moving forward, you can pass those who are stuck in a rut. Those with a negative outlook on life usually end up with negative results; a bad attitude is like a flat tire because you can't get very far until you change it. Paul, through all avenues of his life, remained optimistic and confident in his direction.

Pursuing his passion, Paul became a high school teacher and coach for ten years.

While he was teaching, like many educators because of their unfairly poor salaries, Paul began working in the mortgage industry part time to supplement his income. Because school let out early afternoon, Paul would spend his evenings and weekends smiling and dialing. On his first call, he closed a new client and opened a mortgage for him. While he had early success, it wasn't always that way. With the barrage of rejection came the steadfast determination to prevail. "At that point sales got me excited. Although the ultimate goal was always to make money, it was really in the challenge of becoming a great salesperson and to be able to help somebody that drove me." Paul engrossed himself with personal development to improve his ability to increase his gross sales.

He started making more money part time than his full-time income as a teacher. The realization that he was capable of creating so much more, but not wanting to completely leave his passion, formed a lane shift directing Paul's path toward banking and insurance.

"When you start to get discouraged about what's going on, you need to look for the reinforcement from others who are successful." When you want change, change your approach. Often, that means learning from the best if you want to become better.

While he was growing his book of business in the mortgage industry, he always went above and beyond to serve his clients. During the subprime era, many borrowers had issues with their credit and Paul would do everything possible to assist them in improving their chances for approval. His skill set and knowledge came in handy when he was ready to part ways and start a credit repair company.

Often our greatest shift comes at the intersection of wisdom, experience and chance.

Paul's transition from high school hallways to corporate cubicles, and sweaty gym locker rooms to executive boardrooms, showed him that when one doors closes it may be leading to a window of opportunity.

For Paul, the garage is where his business success got revved up. The first office for Better Qualified, a proven full-service credit restoration company, started in the garage of a mortgage office on Ocean Avenue in Sea Bright, New Jersey. With no heat when they started the company, the weather was manageable, but the winter months were unforgiving. Thankfully, as the temperatures plummeted, their business started heating up and they moved into their first official office space. Despite the location of their facility, their foundation was always built on ethics and superior service.

In the end, talent may get you in the door but character will keep you in the room.

Paul's success as a business leader was facilitated by lessons he learned in his role as a teacher. In the academic world, we are taught lessons and then given a test. In life and the corporate world, we are given tests and we determine the lessons to be interpreted.

In theory, each of his classes was fundamentally a small company, full of pupils who ranged in capability and motivation, with unique hopes and dreams. "I was able to identify those who had goals and not just dreams, but a plan, did the necessary work and excelled within their environment to move on to the next stage of life." From his coaching, Paul observed the correlation between athletic performance, academic accomplishments and the ability to shift and perform at a high level in the working world. Time management, goal setting, teamwork, and the ability to excel as an individual all played a significant role in a student's results. More importantly, as a teacher, Paul's ability to become a pupil and learn how to empower his students created an unparalleled skill that true leaders possess – the ability to motivate each team player to reach their highest potential based on their unique personality. In life, there are many who have natural skills without the work ethic to maximize them, and others who may not be as naturally gifted but maximize their performance through their dedication to excellence.

Paul has built his entire career on bringing out the best in himself to bring out the best in others.

When you focus on your strengths, your business will strengthen. Discipline drove Paul's teaching and coaching and continues to drive his business acumen. Paul shines as a Lane Changer when he's pounding the pavement. His prowess of door knocking and creating strategic partnerships drives the company's achievements while his partner, Eric Michael, focuses on organizational and task-oriented protocol to fuel its dynamic results and keeps them in the right lane.

When Paul made the executive decision to become an executive with his partner and launch the business, he sought counsel from those he respected. Specifically, he approached Steve Meyer, a good friend who owned Advisors Mortgage Group. Much to his dismay, Steve's perception of that industry overshadowed the light that Paul envisioned for his future. Concerned for his friend, Steve encouraged Paul to rethink his direction because most of the people were unethical and walking a thin line legally. "We knew the track record of the people who preceded us was not good. If we just do this the right way and approach it from an honest way, we have 99% of the competition beat," Paul purported. Steve didn't give him his full graces and it burst Paul's bubble. The biggest blessing may have been the simultaneous economic bubble burst because Steve allowed Paul to work on his own personal credit as a test to prove their process and vet his services. Now, with over 55 branches, Steve utilizes Better Qualified constantly for his clients.

Our toughest critics can become are greatest supporters.

When we take the high road, others will want to travel the road with us toward greatness.

Paul's passion for what he does supersedes his need to grind. "Each and every day is a gift. I feel very fortunate because I happen to live my passion." His results in his career reflect who he is as a person. Sitting on the board of the Red Cross and receiving the Good Citizenship award, his community efforts and contribution to society serve as the lifeblood of his success. When we give back, we get so much more.

With a servant attitude for his clients, understanding many of them don't understand the rules of the game, Paul and his team make it an even playing field. It is a constant battle. Being able to fight on behalf of the consumer is the true David and Goliath story; Paul just has the stones to go up against them for his clients. He fights the good fight for those who can't or don't want to with extremely specialized aptitudes. His victories for his clients create champions in their own lives every day. Having Better Qualified on your team gives you the competitive advantage to win the game of life.

At some time in your life you must decide if you want to impress people or influence people. Paul pushed his students because he always pushed himself. He never asked of his students and athletes more than he was willing to do in his own life. When it comes to success and increased performance, we must spend more time with people who bring out the best in us, not the stress in us. When you want to be a champion, play against them. When you have a million-dollar mind, do not surround yourself with one-cent minds. Make the necessary shift.

It becomes necessary to do something you love with complete passion. Work-life balance is essential because short-term success does not always equate to long-term sustainability. We must sacrifice to succeed, but not sacrifice everything to potentially lose everything. We must keep our eye on the ball – our personal priorities and core commitments – if we want to stand on the podium as winners. There are no shortcuts to any place worth going. Sometimes the road of life takes unexpected turns and you have no choice but to follow it to end up in the place you are supposed to be. Other times you must shift gears, pave your own lane and remember that difficult roads often lead to better qualified destinations.

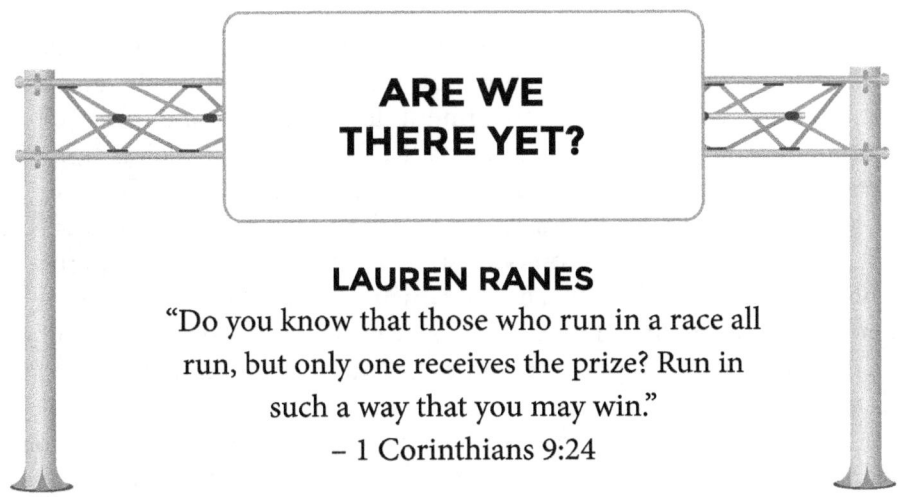

ARE WE THERE YET?

LAUREN RANES

"Do you know that those who run in a race all run, but only one receives the prize? Run in such a way that you may win."
– 1 Corinthians 9:24

    Evaporating seconds pace the beats of my own heart as contagious anticipation builds with the accumulating sea of people around me. Intensity infuses the cool morning air with an indescribable energy on the verge of combustion. I consciously watch the limited bits of shimmering light tickle the ripples on the water's surface, unconsciously taking it all in. Here I am, wading in waiting. I have been stretched to every known limit I have on the way to this moment. Now, I am here, doing my best to unplug from fear, tap into faith, streamline my focus, and visualize the day unwrapping the present of this sought opportunity. The final countdown has begun; we are minutes away from the rest of the day. All the unknown will become known as the day unfolds the untold stories of Ironman, New Zealand. Ready. Set. Almost go time.
Be still. Be present. Just. Be.
T I am not there yet. I am here.

I have never been driven by a destination routed anywhere near easy street and the roads I've chosen to travel often seem to be under construction. Even with the most mindfully marked map, unforeseen detours beyond my control are inevitable. Sometimes, the landscape of life is picturesque, hospitable, and the road rises to meet us whenever we arrive. Other times, we must navigate tangled terrain without the offer of support or an obvious exit strategy to avoid the obstacles that cannot yet be seen from the apex in which we exist. Leading me to believe, when an exit ramp isn't readily available at the time I feel the need to pull off the highway, continuing onto the next exit IS the obvious exit strategy being offered.

No matter what I feel or think I need, we are always given what we really need when we actually need it; good, great, extraordinary, bad, or ugly. God is never late and seldom early, God is always right on time. I am certain of this. Whenever I show up, whatever the agenda inside and around me, I am exactly where I am supposed to be, whenever I arrive. Always. We are living in revision no matter our decisions. It has been a long road and it will be a long way to the other side, beyond the events of life and the forest and the trees. By the grace of God, I will give my best to deliver an on-time arrival of willing and able, at the ready, to take on each day and ride it into tomorrow. Then, maybe I will get some rest. ..

"I have promises to keep, and miles to go before I sleep." -Robert Frost

Shifting Gears

    I made the decision to register for Ironman New Zealand without any prior race experience and not much knowledge of what an Ironman entailed. Revision to every area of my life followed my moment of inspired insanity at Starbucks on 15th Street. Behind all inspired action, there is a why enticing us to move from inspiration to motivation. The why must be moving enough to conjure up the grit to take action, add ample force, and move us through paralysis and analysis, eventually enabling the determination to keep driving in the direction of the dream. Trusting the process with faith in the journey and solid efforts paving the way to eventual domination. There was more than one why in me to fuel the fire I needed to chase my giant across the world. The initial whys had convinced me to sign my life on the line, but most of my whys showed up in their own time. While digesting many miles with training wheels I was introduced to the whys that truly taught me what those miles were about for me.

    If the land of Ironman is as foreign to you as it was to me when I leaped before looking, you will benefit from this breakdown. Ironman consists of a 2.4 mile swim + 112 mile bike ride + 26.2 mile run = 140.6 miles to be completed in less than eighteen consecutive hours on race day. Three disciplines beating meat and feet in a repetitive game of mercy with the mind. I kind of knew that going in, but I intimately KNEW it while I was going through it, and now I understandably KNOW what it really takes to do it. When I registered for this sadomasochism, I thought it was a race against other people. Turns out, I was only ever racing myself. Which may or may not be more sadistic! I have learned that there is Ironman and there is everything else. The beast requires a person to sacrifice as much time, energy, and resources as humanly possible to the fiercest, farthest distance triathlon, appropriately called, Ironman. It is a BIG deal, trust me.

If you don't want to trust my word for it, then trust your journey. Commit to something so big that you will have to grow into the person you need to be in order to reach the other side of the goal post that you cannot yet see or even believe. Experience the uphill battle, grant yourself the power of understanding knowledge through experience, and learn for yourself by coloring on every side of the lines in a similar picture sometime. Knowledge becomes power when we leap into learning, launching ourselves over the ledge, pushing ourselves into the know. Experiential education validates and expands knowledge, in my opinion, becomes, in my experience. The unknown becomes known in the opportunity of the experiential learning journey.

Tenacious exploration of who we are in relation to our environment and personal involvements can expand our personal awareness and perspective, deepening the understanding that can be acquired at the peaks and the valleys of life. Curious intention of personal exploration earns a wealth of experiential lessons drenched with depth. Wisdom is weaved into our mainframe with maximum absorption by stimulating all the senses. Experience is the best teacher because the lesson plans are always naturally unique to the student, and quite often supernaturally exclusive to the student. Ask, and it will be given to you; seek, and you will find; knock, and it will be opened to you. For everyone who asks receives, and he who seeks will find, and to those who knock, it will be opened.

Triathletes are considered and crowned an Ironman on race day but, the Ironman mentality is acquired long before race day, mostly alone during training. During training, It. Gets. Real. The battlefield of the mind ranges without reason and has no boundaries. Highs of feeling desire, passion, pursuit, and lustful wanderings make the juice worth the squeeze. Lows feel lost in wonderings, fears, doubts, and regrets without resolve, always hungry for more aimless thoughts to pick scabs with. Goals, dreams, and fantasies are enveloped in euphoria, wishing and waiting to welcome us back from slaying vampire thoughts that suck our esteem to feed inner demons hiding in the shadows awaiting their time to shine blindness on the brain. Extreme athletes know what it means to battle and conquer inner demons, tame the beasts, and ride reality's potential to the other side of each reach, stretching to shatter the limits that define what is and what can be.

"Everyone says it is impossible until it is done." -Nelson Mandala

Technically, I am ready to power through the day and have a great race. I have successfully executed several hours of professionally coached conditioning and training in the water, on the bike, and on my own two feet. Hours upon hours until exhausted nauseam. Rehearsing for such an event is not like a rehearsal dinner for a wedding, easily unveiling the exact replica of the ceremony soon to follow. Conditioning, training, not even pre-game mock racing can emulate game day in entirety. At the main event, it can be tricky to predict the response of the mind and body plus the connective tissue tying the mind to the body. Athletic endeavors are unpredictable, humbling, and differ one event to the next.

No one knows the struggle, unless the intimacy of the quest has been personally experienced. The common ground all participants stand on is extreme ambition. Ambition capable of paving the road with enough force to push through walls attempting to contain the will to conquer anything in the way. Pushing to and through exhaustion, disciplining desires, forsaking flesh to continually overcome boundaries in a race of mild and massive victories with ourselves, most details known only to the individual. Separated by the many lanes of life, the divided highways of each triathlete have finally merged, paralleling us on an equal playing field of effort to stretch the limits of the skin we are in.

Keeping my mind calm and my body steady is proving to be a worthy challenge the unique morning of my main event. Wearing a blank stare, I silently waged war with uninvited, unwelcome worries, burning the time that I could be spending in prayer to edify the encouragement needed to paddle passed the prison song of my own mind's discouraging tone. I entertained the original plan of staying the course, of course. I also entertained the idea of blowing this popsicle stand and eat sweets every mile on the road to the land of Far, Far Away. I fantasized farfetched scenes of evasion including but not limited to piranha swarms, fresh water land sharks, alien invasion complete with random abduction, massive diddymo infestation followed by lake evacuation, chemical leak overtaking the air and water in the lake, oil spill doing the same, volcanic eruption, earthquake and lake draining, T-virus infected zombie triathletes, the classic act of a bomb threat, or simply faking an injury.

Why would I want to run from this after spending so much time, money, and distance running toward this? I don't know. Then again, I am still identifying all the reasons why I came to race in the first place. I have extensively, relentlessly trained my body and my mind is paralyzed by the blunt force realization that this commitment is so much bigger than anything I have ever endured. Stifled with fears in the dark dawn at the start of this day, my own insecurities batter me with doubt that didn't exist a month ago. Quietly questioning, "am I ready? Am I all set? Am I really ready to go?" Not like those three question marks even matter now. Go time waits for no one, countless opportunities have been lost to irrational hesitation. Either you jump in and go after it or you hold back and don't go at all.

"If you think you can do a thing...or think you can't do a thing, you're right." - Henry Ford

Somewhere between stage fright, fear, and silly scenes of Ironman exodus, faith that I couldn't seem to find sooner, showed up in my defense. Nudging me with the reminder to go inside, take refuge, find focus, and let yourself go with the flow of the day. I was created by God, for God, and all things work together for good. The Ironman and medal awarded at the finish line is a bitty part of why I am here in New Zealand and here on earth, in this skin that I am in. No matter what happens, it will happen for me, to further my evolution and my relationship with Jesus Christ, the truth of all life's whys and why nots. On my own, I am not enough to conquer all the extraordinary things put on my heart, all the extraordinary things I was created to inspire and achieve. It is God that takes me and makes me, gives to me and works through me, enabling my abilities to support my desires in a race with faith and nothing to lose except time. I have waited on the Lord, my strength has been renewed, I will run and not grow weary, and I will walk and not grow faint. In that moment, I found myself on solid ground through faith strong enough to dwarf fear and move me through all the mountains around me.

I am here.

At the ready.

Faced with the here and now.

Nothing before this moment matters.

Nothing beyond this moment matters.

Nothing matters more than this moment.

Shifting Gears

The sound of the cannon blast initiates a field of feet propelling thousands of meat machines into the deep demands waiting on the horizon. Just like that, and they're off. I stood still in the waist high water, watching the frantically finning feet, pausing to sip a breath, savoring the seconds left on this side of the starting line. One last gulp of air, moving my focus to breathing, simultaneously encouraging myself to be mindfully present before getting lost in the cadence of the day. Pushing planted feet out from under me, I plunge deeper than the surface and the tape is torn on the biggest hurdle of the day...and I'm off.

I kicked and I got kicked, I splished and I splashed, I zigged and I zagged, I cried and I cramped, I swam every stroke created by man and beast and added salty tears to that fresh water lake. 2.4 miles is a lot to cover in water, I felt every inch of that distance by the wrap of the lap. I almost couldn't believe that I touched down on the lake bottom as I approached the shoreline. I was dizzy but vertical and grateful a leg cramp didn't land me face down on the path of the sandy shore as I exiled myself from the lake! I was ecstatic that I did not sink and that counts as a swim, plus I wrung myself out of the lake in time to be considered a completed competitor of the Ironman swim. Smiling my way through the dissipating crowd, I owe myself a hug and a personal ovation of pats on the back for defeating the swim before the swim defeated me. First obstacle on the course wrapped. Next up, transition to 112 miles on a bike.

Giddy up.

The transition area is a tented execution of athletes unwrapping themselves from wet gear to slip into something more comfortable and appropriate to navigate the ride of a cycle built for speed. Just a short session to shed what has already been purposed, and reset while gearing up to push on through to the other side of the transformation tent. Transitions and transition areas of life last much longer than the volunteer assisted mini magic quick-change trick of a triathlon transition. I primped and prepared to mount my carbon stallion, slapping on my cycling gear, shoving fuel into the me machine. Feeling something between yay and nay with the lump in my tummy quickly dissolving what was left of the skin on my teeth and my will to keep up with the pace of the race...but I was still in it.

Hustling to shift disciplines without grinding gears, I galloped my bike onto the track, reflecting my swim with commentary in my head for kicks and giggles,"...check out Lauren swim against all odds on the 2015 blooper reel." Seriously though, I am embarrassed that I barely delivered myself to the swim finish line in time. My breath stroke flipped into a backstroke and eventually rolled over into a delirious dog paddle for the grand finale of my approach. This is Ironman, the best of the beast people throw down on this course and I puppy paddled to shore. How did that happen? Inspiration often comes with tragedy. Striving to stay positive, choosing to be happy, topped with the activation of my sixth sense of humor put the foundation back under me and birthed another wind for me to ride with. I found a laugh to adjust my smile for the cheering supporters standing by for my flyby of shame. Many without a horse in the race, the volunteers, locals, and encouraging spectators, make this event possible with immense support and a shared desire to see each individual conquer themselves all the way to the finish line.

After just a bit of peddling I caught up with the pack, much easier to go with the flow when the other tricyclers on the road are within my scope to be seen and gauged. When surrounding traffic seems to be smoothly cruising life in the fast lane, it appears everyone has been given directions more accurately descript than my own. Even if that is the case, it is still best to look forward, keep eyes on the road, stay in your lane, and do your best to peripherally pace the passengers passing through life alongside of you. Life will not slow down when a rest stop is needed by any one person, riding the road of Ironman is the same. If you do slow down or ride to the side for a break, no matter how brief the break, it will be paid for in time. We must adapt to the ever-changing pace of living, keeping on and keeping up with one day to the next. As much as we are all in this together, we were all born our own being, ultimately racing ourselves on a track all our own within the collective course of the human race.

Shifting Gears

I was active and fit prior to putting on my training wheels for Ironman, that didn't matter much every time I couldn't unclip from my pedals before toppling into the unforgiving concrete streets. Ironman was created for super stud people but maybe best if left to be pursued by Tony Stark and almost all other super heroes, some super villains, most Greek gods, few urban legends, hungry cheetahs, and the gazelles those big cats are in pursuit of. I am none of the above. All those fierce enough to mount the challenge are welcome to join, but this race was not designed with the average Jane or Joe in mind. When flat foot Jane does compete, her race will not look like the scenes shown in victorious clips of completion. Or defeat for that matter. The average Jane will give all she can give, empty the reserves and look like she went all in for every bit of that race. Nothing like the iron chicks in the clips snipped from the finish line, looking the same coming out as they did going in. Those incredible athletes have not only worked hard, but make amazing look even better. I have the utmost respect for the beauty, build, athleticism, and all the other attributes they deserve credit for. The details and extent of each athlete's journey will vary, but the workload and the challenging special brew of insanity it takes to play this game is all relative. Some super stars just look so good doing it. Cheers to you, Iron ladies and gentlemen.

Every day, the sunshine rises with another take of the greatest movie always being made: Life. We may be the director of our own lifetime story, but we are not in complete control of our life or the time of our lives. Ironically, we aren't out of control either. We may be driving the car when the scenery starts moving around us but we are not the only car on the road and we certainly cannot be the road that always knows where it is going. We are all cruising within a kind of collaborative controlled traffic that requires steering with a grip on control issues. With all the variables of life, control cannot be fully grasped, you cannot hold onto something you have never fully had a hold of. All control except self-control is an illusion churning and turning the dirt on the path to quick sand, keeping us from accelerating to the speed we need to achieve the footing to prepare the placement of the next step.

Consistently matching will with ability is the secret to sustaining stamina. Mastering that practice is much more challenging than I imagined. It's harder than it appears to chain the pedal to the metal with repetitive action and avoid running an empty tank on fumes into a road block! I have abused the empty indicator line in my personal fuel gauge by taking on too much to work with fuel fumes! Riding the red line moves me forward as intended, but when I continually run in the red for too long I find that the option of shifting gears becomes mandatory. Balancing all areas of life is crucial for optimal health and performance. I have learned the hard way that imbalance is the precursor to burn out just before flaming out and crashing the car into the wall that I built! Above all else, it is important that we drive our lives fully fueled, starting with healthy habits to thrive the entire drive. Simply said, not so simply implemented when working with a timeless design, a sticky processor, an internal operating system seemingly programmed to work against objectives, no IT department to assist with the bugs in this intricately complex man machine, and a designer that empowers your executive decision-making skills.

Endurance requires awareness of the vehicle being driven plus the driver's attention to the details necessary to sustain the vehicle, especially when the driver is that vehicle. Deliberate action including premeditation is essential to keep steady momentum, and ultimately qualify for completion of the task at hand. The mind gives out before the body, staying encouraged is an essential ingredient. This can keep doubt from baking a cake for a pity party tentatively scheduled to take place just about the time you find yourself riding the sidelines of the race. Fold staples of training into a batter, beat and blend to desired consistency, use personal thrust plus tail wind to hold tight within the fast lane when able. Mix in the contrast of knowing when to down shift to keep feet beating when a slower flow is all you can go.

I was feeling so deficient and sick at the beginning of the race. It did not get better but I kept rocking that smile from the beginning to the end of each mile. Sometimes all you can offer is a smile. Perhaps that smile is the crown representing the success already achieved, the success that can be achieved and recalled in each moment of exasperation on the way to reach the next aspiration. There was no life guard on duty to handle the swim for me! The bike ride was eating me alive, mentally and physically. I was heavy everywhere, inside and outside. I was seduced by the smell of a steak dinner the night before the big race and I RARELY eat red meat. Terrible timing to integrate a change to my nutrition and carry a hard to digest boulder around in my belly on race day! What was happening on the inside was not easily seen from the outside though. It's my race, mine to me. For celebratory victory as well as death wishing misery. I don't need to bleed bad seeds into my surroundings with anything that is trying to surround me on the inside, it's bad enough I know what's happening backstage behind the drawn curtain.

The road to achieving any goal is messy and challenging. The view from the peak expands the vision and reminds us how far we have come, encouraging the next place we will go. Traveling the valley of the shadow of trees accommodates claustrophobia, encouraging the discouraging thought of going nowhere fast. The ebbs and the flows are exhausting, emotional, and very real. Goals cemented in commitment and sealed with the mortar of a measurable timeline will reel in reality and burst the bubble of the fantasy to reveal our point on the map and strengthen our navigation captain skillset for mapping the road ahead. Vow to overcome obstacles, in sickness and in health, accept and be present with the here and now, and do your best to never question what waits for around the bend. No matter what, when, how, who, or where, revelation meets us on the road. We will always be on our way to the next place we are going, with or without goals set in stone. Might as well set some mile marking goals in stone. To take the training wheels off and ride until goals are reached, fix your focus wherever you are. Putting best efforts of preparation in place is not a guarantee you will succeed, Certainty will not be found anywhere except the finish line. Even the pros know, preparation does not always equal domination.

"The will to succeed is important, but what's more important is the will to prepare." -Bobby Knight

Time management, strategic organization, machine maintenance, encompassed by a narrow scope of focus can trample and triumph whatever we set our systems to pursue. Still, there is no insurance to cover the lapse of judgment, lapse of memory, lack of energy, or lack of time. On the lap back to transition into a full marathon run, I started wonder if the high demand and investment costs of this Ironman feat are really worth it in the end. Depends who you ask. What is the wear and tear on my mind, body, and life really worth? I thought about all the training I had endured for the endurance of this race, all the work I had horse powered through. This one day alone was worth far more than a towel, a medal, and a speaker saying, "Lauren Ranes, you are an Ironman" (reveling in your victory, but move over so the next athlete can be crowned!) My riding mind thought, there should be something more substantial waiting at the end of this distance and dedication. Like an around the world trip or a super sensational spa day to relax, recover, and recalibrate. Even for the not so spectacular tri-stars like myself, who have stayed the course and carried the weight. Wait. I am on an around the world trip in gorgeous, unique, New Zealand, and I am riding my bike in circles? For a towel and a title to validate my ability to persevere to a break through or a breaking point? This is my prize for pushing through to the other side! I have persevered to overcome countless times; I was my witness every time! My opinion matters most to me and only God can judge me. I don't need this and no one needs me more than I need me now.

God must have heard my thoughts as a request for reprieve, because a recovery vehicle driven by a "failed" Ironman competitor of the past pulled up beside me to talk about the weather. Before I realized it, I had chucked my bike and myself into the opportunity of being driven back to where this all started. That's when my race placed before I gave myself the opportunity to reach the finish line. Sitting upright, air conditioning in my face was great just before the self-loathing reality sunk in.
I disqualified myself. "Lauren Ranes, you are NOT an Ironman" after all that.

The ironic part is, I was thinking of me and my wellbeing, but more so considered everyone else that I may be letting down and they probably couldn't care less, because everyone alive is primarily focused on their own lives. I didn't think I had let myself down by falling short. On the contrary, I thought I had done myself a favor in my moment of weakness. Every weakness is perfectly paralleled as a strength. Weakness sharpens strength and vice versa. Acknowledging one without the other is to sweep sand to the sea. Quitting was not a weakness. Choosing to take care of myself and enjoy my life outside of everything Ironman was a strength. I wasn't that I thought I couldn't reach the finish line, I just didn't think the juice (of completion) was worth the squeeze (of stress on every part of me) anymore.

Just like that Ironman started to feel like a soup sandwich on a stick and I was the one paying and falling apart. That just sounds like it costs too much and doesn't make much sense. Where the mind goes, the body will follow. Once the mind truly decides, that decision cannot be broken. That's how I got here in the first place! My number one is me, I'm not beating myself up or down for anyone or anything. Chasing the promise of momentary victory is not worth wearing and tearing myself up and down. I halted the physical fight yet continued to beat myself up mentally and emotionally the whole ride back to the starting point! Thanks to my detour driver and my decision to save myself a personal power trip, I made it back to the recovery tent way faster than some of the other triathletes I blazed trails with.

I stepped off the recovery vehicle and walked into the recovery tent, observing all the beautiful bodies that have undergone a long day of personally inflicted punishment. It was then that it hit me. I made a choice to sacrifice the investment in myself to save myself from myself. For that moment, the remorse of my self-administered disqualification melted away and I felt peace. I am not professional athlete. Burning up my body for an investment not even close to being worth as much as I am worth, is clearly not worth it. Even if I was a professional, paid to repeatedly compete in this feat around the world, would the physical, mental, and financial sacrifices be worth it in the end? I don't know, that's not my story. I do know I am tenacious and that's a strength. I am also stubborn and that can be a weakness. Different sides of the same coin adding up to basically the same thing. I don't give up easily. I hold on until fingers fall off, I run until my paws bleed, adhere until my heart breaks to pieces. I chose to let go of the vision of victory and I chose to hold onto myself. I am priceless. No one gets to beat me down, especially not me. That is the day I chose to accept me outside the lines, inside the lines, left of center and far from the right. I am just me and that is all I need to be, today and always.

However, after exploring New Zealand, I was back to reality on my side of the pond.

I spent the following months cycling through recovery, trying to support myself as nemesis thinking gave me all the reasons why I am pathetic for failing the finish line. A part of me believed I let myself down, I still believed I let others down, I believed people were disappointed in me, I believed that I didn't measure up, I believed all the resources were in vain, and I believed that I burned through time with wasted energy spinning me in circles of effort, ultimately leading to a failed mission. My ego swelled from hits of stinging shrapnel. I listened to every lie flying at me from where I sat behind my own enemy lines. Images of Ironman pulled me down into a vast expansion of regrettable memories, showcasing all the things that I remember about things I still want to forget.

All the people who believed in my ability and supported me through every journey.

All the time, money, and effort invested for nothing.

All the training I have fought my way through.

All the words of the people who have been in my shoes.

Shifting Gears

All the mountains I didn't think my faith could move.
All the times I bit off more than I could chew.
All the passion I have ever pursued to pointlessly conclude.

    I fixated myself in a make-believe bankruptcy and I marinated in the basement of my breakdown long enough to snuff the light out and cry out for the sun to shine on me again. I felt raped, robbed, and pillaged. I struggled to get in touch with the girl I formerly knew and loved before the events in New Zealand. All the pre-existing pain from the past that I had already sorted and stored on the shelf of self, caught up with me in my drained vacancy, rendering me helpless to assist any sort of accent from this indescribable emptiness. My heart was on the verge of collapse.

    My joy was unreachable. My motives were mandatory but void of matter to me. Destitute desires kept conversations and commitments with family, friends, and colleagues. Opportunities to lift others up did little to impact the gravitational pull on my broken spirit. I wasn't answering roll call, I rented the master bedroom inside of me to a doppelgänger.

    Once vibrant and inviting, shielding myself became my new normal, almost unbeknownst even to me. Forced interaction with everyday responsibilities became a way of life. I withheld myself, cloaked within a presentation of fake smiles and lazy listening, careful not to share the weight I was wearing with anyone that crossed my path. Behind closed doors, my captive mind ate me alive until I overflowed onto my knees in prayer, crying out for the sun to shine again. Regularly seeking the solace of a solo space to bathe myself in self-centered hugs as deep breaths followed tears down my cheeks. With the banner around my mind day and night, "please, Lord don't let it be in vain."

I tried to return to training. Too soon. Things that I used to enjoy and nothing. Still, I evaded me. I discovered what the greyhounds must feel when the rabbit they chase always remains just out of reach. I clawed my way through everyday biting my lip to cut into a new kind of pain. Day turned to night as it does, and I walked off stage to sleep with my dreams by the palm trees. I downshifted to a standstill. Time is ticking with the revolving reality that nothing ever truly stands still. People, places, and things are always either appreciating or depreciating. Materializing or deteriorating. Ascending or Descending. Moving forward or falling behind. I consciously knew logic and reason but had not yet accepted it all on an unconscious level. This too shall pass, this too is meant to be or it would not have been. I knew deep, deep inside, by God, by God's grace, nothing is in vain. All the pieces that had broken off while I was behind the curtains breaking down, were finding their way into the new parts of my heart still sore from being blasted open. Healing is a lifelong song, I am adaptable and I am progressing perfectly.
Truth.

This is a chapter in my life, a blip in time. You are reading a chapter about my life, an even smaller blip in your life. I thought this would be an easy, fun, creative process with a twist and a twinge of discomfort looking back on the past. I didn't know all that would come with these lines. This is not fun, this is not easy, and this has taken me as much as I have had to give to it. Life happened around me, finding time and peace of mind to continue writing has been the most recent feat. Well, sometimes you don't get to find the time, you inadvertently make time when the time finds you. This segment of my story is brought to you via bed rest. I burned out the red line through every area of my life, neglecting myself as the sacrifice to work through the to do list of life around me. So many whispering reasons why I have thought about dropping my contribution out of this book. About as many times as I considered disqualifying myself from the race I am recalling for you. Life presents whys and wise contingencies.

This is not about Ironman. It often isn't about what you think it is going to be about, and it's not always about you. We live in our heads and we know ourselves better than anyone ever will. Except God, God knows everything and more. It is so easy to be self-absorbed; everyone's favorite subject is their own story. We lived it and wrote it and to the best of our knowledge and ability, it is accurate enough for us to confidently share the details. Though, I know this story better than anyone, I am not confident sharing the details. I don't want to share. It's not a victory lap and it's not a sad scene of a shamed past. I generally like to whittle words, this has not been a fun short write and it's not a feel-good story. Not for me anyway. This is not easy to talk about, let alone write about. I am good at compartmentalizing, especially pain and strain my heart and soul have sustained. I am even better at internalizing everything, reanimating all the ways it went wrong. To deal with the unpleasantries of the past, I get in it and I get dirty with it and I get out of it by getting on with it. I dissect and decipher until tapering understanding into a container that fits snugly into the compartment that was carved while I was deep in the den of dissemination. Then I move on without the weight of yesterday, only checking the rear view to be sure it stays behind me, carefully cruising passed the opportunity to relive or recreate a similar scenario.

I know this the hard part. The part that softens the lump I never allow to make itself known, even to me. I am fighting not to fight it. I am riding the tears rolling down my cheeks, writing and reliving all the events that have passed into past tense. I have missed a lot and it will stay missing from me. I am reminiscing more of the past than I will ever put to pages. So why would I want to share? I already told you, I don't want to share. I do not want to share any of this with you or anyone else for that matter. I don't want anyone knowing me, let alone people I don't know! It's not me, it's for you and it's not you, it's for me. Perhaps only I fully understand that, thanks to the voice that won't shut up about this story. I have gotten engulfed in more than one life story of lessons and leisure listening to this voice of rationally irrational reasoning. This story doesn't want to stay inside, so I'm letting the cat out of its bag.

We tailor our tale, no one knows life behind our eyes and we don't even know all our reasons why, humanity is too complex to completely understand, even as a human! Life is lived forward, but better understood when observed backward. Whether we literally write or not, we are the pen and we write from the inside out not the other way around. Life happens within us, around us, and I believe everything that happens in our life, happens for us. To teach us, to reach us, to teach us to reach higher, to reach others, to try harder, lighten up and soften the blow of the direct hits we get lit up with in life. A relationship with truth will light your way with clarity and wisdom, providing protection from lurking things that go unnoticed, waiting to trip us up and slow us down. We are all stronger than we know and everyone has a purpose for being born into this life, for being here, now. The only deadline in life is the day your heart stops beating with the pace of the breath in your lungs. If you ask, look, and listen, you will find the way, the truth, and the light for your path.

Only God can judge me. No person can certify, judge, or credit anyone as a failure, as a loser, a short comer, a tail dragger, whatever lying label chosen to demean individual importance. We will never be losers and we cannot fail in life. Only misalign with goals and expectations. Falling short or even falling face down on the path is one way to truly measure the distance and drive inside to reach achievement. We can't lose and we can't fail to win. The only thing that we are ever really losing is time and time is ticking quickly. Spend more time than money on nouns that cannot be bought. This is the best investment we can make while we still have time to spend. Everyone gets to be who they are and who they are becoming. I believe, we are all meant to make more and be more than the money we make.

Our reputation is how others see us. Our identity is what we tell ourselves to be true of who we are and what we are made of, our value system shapes how we see the world around us, and how we value ourselves will affect the shape of the world we contribute to creating. Others can see our potential and we should fan the flames of the potential we see in others. We can always encourage and edify the potential in others to materialize and grow. Unfortunately, there seems to be discouragement in the faces we share space with, often more than encouragement affirming capability.

"Losers" of the race face just as many, if not more feats and victories than the MVP, these are the unsung heroes that we don't hear enough from. Star quality machines of men and women amaze with superhuman ability shooting from the seams of these super humans. We expect amazing from these types and I appreciate super freak athletes in any game frame. I have come to truly admire the overworked, underpaid, underqualified, overweight, food addicted, bad pattern participating, newcomer or overcomer running against the wind of all odds, just a little bit more. These underdogs boast a certain awe-inspiring kind of impressive. I used the skin on my teeth to come in short of the finish line, arriving a failure from the point of view only focused on the goal of the timed finish line. Three thousand, four hundred, fifty sixth place walks away without a medal, but walks with the humility and the courage to accept, embrace, and shine in a different way.

I look back upon it all; God's been merciful to me all along. I don't know how I rallied and did what I to do to get thru each day of training. I don't know how I got my head right to create enough force to empty an already exhausted fuel tank. Since I'm letting it all hang out, I still don't quite understand why I even signed up for the race. 0.01% of the world population successfully completes an Ironman. I had never done a triathlon before, not a duathlon, not a marathon, not a half marathon, not a color run, a fun run, nor an xterra adventure race. Dating back to school days, I had never completed or even had interest in doing a race of any kind. The only race that I remain interested in is, The Amazing Race around the world, and that's about the adventure. I don't care for swimming and clearly, I don't have a talent for swimming. I haven't really ridden a bike since the handlebars had streamers and I pretended the bike was a unicorn. I don't have the best feet or hips for running, nor is running my favorite form of exercise. Though I am equipped for many physical demands, I am not necessarily structurally sound enough to engage a 3 discipline survival of the fittest without some kind of fall out. Yet, I joined up with the fiercest athletes in their element. Breaking down the mechanics and sweating it out with the intimidating yet disarming athletes of Breakaway Training, wrapping laps and getting lapped by the most ferocious fleet of triathletes on the planet.

I cannot explain all my reasons why, I do understand from my core to my pores though. Everyone can use a jaunt outside of the normal routine of life to jump into an unfamiliar adventure, it keeps life interesting and prevents rust and dust from settling on us, plus it's a good way to keep away from the caution tape of complacency. A state of complacency is inaccurately described as a "comfort zone". Comfort zones are not comfortable and complacency is far from contentment. In fact, "comfort" zones are so uncomfortable that desperate measures are often taken to escape overstaying the revolving welcome. Familiar is the best definition of the zone that keeps us from being all we aspire to be. We can become accustomed to familiarity, the familiar zone can be complacent, but it is not comfortable. Only you know what you're made of. The more you step outside of the known and push yourself beyond the familiar zone and into the unpredictable zone of the unknown, the more you will know what you're made of. All things considered, I did ok for being an unlikely Ironman contending triathlete, and I wasn't alone. All sizes, shapes, and colors took to the water, the cycle, and the road on my race day and every other race day all over the world.

I still struggle to grant myself the freedom to accept what is meant to be when the rubber meets the road, both then and now. I am a work in progress, allowing myself the ease to receive reality however it shows up, a bit more every day. I am learning that it is ok to sit back, relax, enjoy the ride, and observe the collision of life experience and collateral beauty. The past has lapsed, the future is on the way as each passing second becomes the past. Time is the most valuable commodity and the most invaluable gift that can be given or received. Though we can sell the time we have in the days of our lives, we cannot purchase more minutes on the clock. Every arriving moment is an incoming gift of time, naturally absorbed by the gift of the present. Time consistently keeps pace with its own cadence, never speeding or slowing for any reason outside of its own existence. No matter the speed of my steps, I can only take one step at a time and the most important step is always the step that I am on.

My smile never left me after my desire to keep racing was long gone because we are all sucking up a struggle in one way or another. The smile I wear on my face every day reflects what will never change. Everyone counts. Even the contenders that didn't measure up to the standards of the race or whatever the matters we may face throughout the human race with life. Everyone matters. Everything matters. The smallest effort or smile can lighten the load of the burden attempting to build boundaries bigger than the fact that we can better overcome obstacle together. I believe with every bit of me that we were all created by God, for God. God is bigger than anything we can wrap our minds around. Believe and seek the Lord with any amount of faith that can be mustered, you will find that Jesus is Lord and God is everything.

We are all thoughtfully purposed to be here, no matter how short timelines and interaction may be. I also believe that people are the only eternal creation. Be light enough to lift others, edifying ourselves as we build people around us up, the burden is light when lifted up. Only the affirmation of encouragement can stoke the fire of the phoenix. Each one of us has the God given power to call out the champion in every person we meet. Step out and step up to bring the champion out in others. Our words and our actions have power beyond our imagination, the power build up or tear down. When words build, worlds are built up, there is no limit to how far that effect can stretch. Ripples make waves, it's time to make waves roll as far as they can go while we are here and while we are on the way there to the next place we go.

That's the short of the long story about Lauren Ranes of California accepting and becoming more than an Ironman. The time when I gave up, gave out, gave in, gave everything to God and found peace and victory within the crash and road rash. Ashes traded for the beauty of lessons learned from forms of failure I've endured. Prayers in the name of Jesus are never in vain, His word will not return void. May my words be used to empower efforts and inspire others to recover and rise up on wings as eagles with renewed strength, seeking more than they could fathom before the moment they found their wings. So, back to the original question, when we do get there, are we there yet? Nope. We can go "there" but we can never truly be "there" even when we do get there, we are here once again. There we go and here we are, getting wherever we are headed, one step at a time. We will arrive on time, then, there will once again become here as the present chases the future into the past.

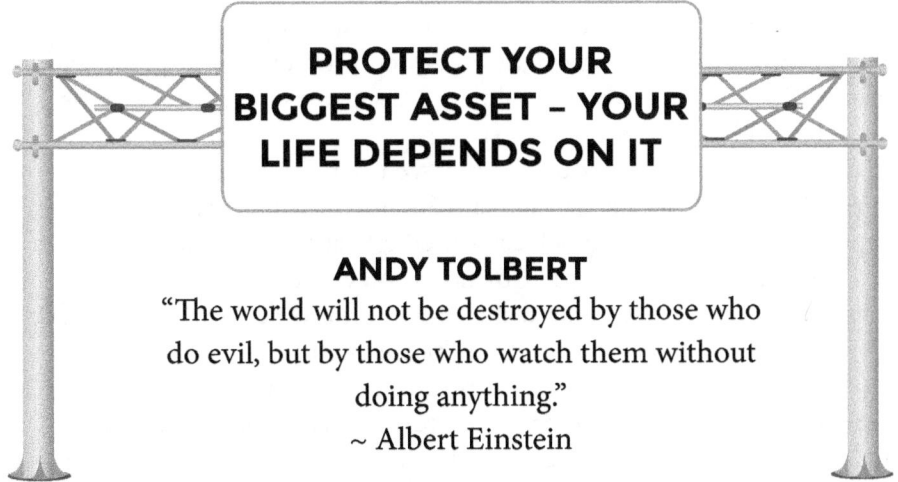

PROTECT YOUR BIGGEST ASSET – YOUR LIFE DEPENDS ON IT

ANDY TOLBERT

"The world will not be destroyed by those who do evil, but by those who watch them without doing anything."
~ Albert Einstein

Life is either a daring adventure or nothing at all, but along the journey we must be prepared because when we let our guard down, we become susceptible to attacks. You will become safe not because of the absence of danger, but because of the presence of your best self. Taking risks is dangerous, but playing safe doesn't allow you to know your true capability. Successful people take big risks knowing that they might fall hard; but they might succeed more than they ever fantasized. Nothing is impossible to those who dream; nothing is unobtainable to those who strive; nothing is unreachable to those who dare to reach out.

Growing up, Andy Tolbert's parents owned a gun store. Being around that lifestyle and spending countless hours at the range began her lifelong interest in self-defense and firearms. It was simply part of her nature.

But that didn't make them invincible. Their home was burglarized multiple times and their family store was robbed. The burglars tied up the employees in the back office and proceeded to steal much of their inventory.

In life and business, there are times when life gets out of control. In those moments of helplessness, we must rely on our instincts and training to protect us. While we can't control everything, we must learn to control what we can. When you learn self-control, you can master anything.

Their family made slight shifts by installing alarm systems and even getting a family Doberman for added protection and preservation of their home. Although she didn't realize it as a child, these events have shaped her life and her lifestyle.

While we pursue our dreams, we open ourselves to vulnerability that others can take advantage of. It becomes our responsibility to equip ourselves at the highest level to take advantage of any situation and turn it in our favor. Never let your emotions overpower your intelligence; we do not want moments of temporary distress to force us to do something permanently foolish.

We do what we must, in order to enjoy our lives fully and completely. The reality is that no matter how equipped we are to survive life, none of us can escape death.

Andy sadly lost her father to cancer when she was 11.

She discovered the best protection any woman can have is massive courage.

Shortly after, her family relocated from a rural part of Florida to Sarasota, a higher-end beach community. You can take the girl out of the country but you can't take the country out of the girl. Andy's mom opened an English tack store selling riding equipment and horse supplies, partly as a way to teach her what her father didn't get a chance to. Andy saddled up and played valuable roles in the business from attending buying trips to doing inventory, and she was responsible for all the marketing and advertising.

Andy's experience in her parent's gun store, along with their other ventures, armed her for practices most adults, let alone children, wouldn't have the privilege of gaining.

"It's all I ever knew so I don't know how it would be different any other way."

With an entrepreneurial spirit, she took her earnings from working in the family store and opened a jewelry shop within the store to sell horse-themed fine jewelry. She was solely responsible for the success or failure of the business. "You learn about pricing decisions, budgeting and forecasting. If you work in a large retail store, you only learn one aspect because it's compartmentalized for you. In the family business, I had to figure out how all the roles interplayed."

I guess you could say if she were to have a 'Gallup' poll about her success as a businesswoman, she was hot out the GAIT!

"I've always been that type of person. I didn't have a first word as a baby; I had a first sentence - 'All by self," Andy confirms. "Tell me what needs to be done and I'll figure it out. I don't need a whole lot of direction."

This mentality and approach has served as a pro and a con. In one way, her get-it-done attitude creates phenomenal results. On the other hand, sometimes by not asking for help, she may not solve a problem that could have led to even more significant outcomes. "What you struggle through to figure out, somebody may have been able to fix for you, but only if you ask and only if you let them," she encourages.

When you can't handle the Clydesdale, pony up and let others help you.

Many of us horse around in our business and treat them like hobbies. Until you take full ownership, develop yourself as the person you need to achieve the success you desire, understand your strengths and weaknesses, shift your focus and energy, you remain trotting toward disaster instead of cantering toward greatness.

Andy has always created success. She confidently trusts whatever field she enters, she will prosper.

"In business, time is money," Andy confirms. "Now, when I can, I pay someone to come in and get it done faster. When we do things on our own we think it will save us time and money, but may cost us more in the long run. Even when you can, maybe you shouldn't."

One of the best ways to determine where your time and energy should be spent is to identify your strengths and weaknesses. Those areas in which you aren't as proficient, find someone who's strong in those to do them for you. "If it's a hobby business, you can probably do it all yourself. If you truly want to build a business that is self-sustaining, and can support you long-term, you cannot do it all."

Circumstantially, Andy took the entrepreneurial path not just because it was the better option, it was the obvious one. When she was preparing to graduate from college she attended the university's job fair, but most of the employers hadn't shown up. Over half the tables were empty. The job market was desolate.

Andy recognized the fastest way to cash was selling. She sold everything from copy machines to embroidered clothing, ultimately finding her niche in the mortgage industry when she was placed at a firm by a headhunting company.

"What I discovered in hours-for-dollars jobs is you don't necessarily get promoted and paid more because you do better work. There were many times I was working smarter and harder than everyone else but because they were older and more experienced they made more money."

Like a farm with horses, companies often dangle a carrot in front of us to encourage and motivate us to keep going to help their bottom line. But the REAL bottom line is that until you commit to your own goals and dreams, you will always be building someone else's.

"I like being rewarded by results and performance," Andy boasts.

When she began building her mortgage book of business, networking at local REIAs for leads, she discovered the possibility and profitability on the flip-side of the real estate businesses. She began flipping houses with her husband, relying on her knowledge and training from running and operating the family businesses. Andy and her husband, Tim, opened their own mortgage company. Right out the gate, they were off and running.

Operating a business with a significant other, or any partner, presents unique challenges. Dividing and conquering becomes essential. You must remain in your lane and focus on accomplishing your agenda and responsibilities. Each person's success or failure affects the overall success or failure of the business. You must pick your battles in the fight to succeed.

With newfound success in their industry, Andy started teaching investment courses to new investors on how to flip houses. She also led education classes for realtors about the ever-changing market. She seemed to pioneer her way to progress. Before they were commonplace, Andy would lead bus trips through neighborhoods to teach and educate aspiring investors how to capitalize in one of the best wealth-building strategies.

She found home in teaching others how to buy and sell houses.

"When you can find something that you love doing, and it's helping other people, and you can make a pretty good living at it too, you've hit your trifecta. There's a lot of personal satisfaction I get when someone succeeds from what I taught them."

When we follow the path that leads to greatness, we can help others get on the right track, too. Moreover, the road to success may merge with a new opportunity that completely changes our lives, and the lives of those we can impact.

Andy was constantly networking and associating with other investors. Their leads became her diamonds in the rough. But often, they were in rough neighborhoods. Specifically, she and Tim visited a foreclosed home in Daytona Beach, a city an hour away that they were unfamiliar with. When they arrived, the combination lock code didn't work. As they were walking around the property from the outside, peering through a window, another set of eyes were staring directly back at Andy from the inside. A homeless man, who was squatting in the house, became a vessel of awareness and direction for them. More importantly, he forced a moment of reflection for Andy and Tim. During their interaction with the squatter, he began pointing out other boarded-up, distressed homes. They hadn't even recognized the type of neighborhood they were entering because they were so focused on one address that they weren't paying attention to their surroundings. Intentional focus is the driver of success, but we also must use our side view mirrors on the road of life to keep us and those around us safe.

This became one of Andy's biggest downshifts ever and caused her to slow down and assess.

She often went to look at houses on her own. The only reason Tim was there was because it was far away. What if she had been alone? What if the lock had worked and she walked in on a scary situation? What if the man had been on drugs and attacked?

When we make ourselves vulnerable and susceptible to our environment, it becomes much more necessary to be able to protect ourselves. Investing is risky, but we don't want it to be dangerous and potentially deadly. You can always lose money on a deal but you don't want to lose your life in the process.

Their personal experience, along with learning about other's perilous experiences, directly encouraged Andy and Tim to form a company educating investors and realtors how to protect themselves during some of the most exposed moments of their lives. They couldn't conceal their knowledge anymore; it was time to lock and load in a new arena!

She merged her knowledge of self-defense, her passion for teaching and her experience and success in the real estate world from various positions to form a life-saving company for real estate professionals.

The perfect trifecta.

Her company, Safer Agent, is dedicated to helping real estate agents and other real estate professionals keep both themselves and their customers safer in the field. It is essential you understand what they teach; your life literally depends on it.

Andy humbly understands the importance of her work. She doesn't do it for the glamor but has the guts to do it for the glory of others. She doesn't know all the lives she may have saved, but she is driven by the fact that more realtors die in the field every year than firefighters. It also truly hits close to home because one of her best friends was abducted by a client while she was at work. After a lunch meeting as they were walking to their cars, he offered to drive her to her car. Rather than escorting her to the car, he proceeded to exit the restaurant parking lot. As was driving to his house encouraging her to loosen up and have a drink with him, Andy's friend, relying on her knowledge from Safer Agent, convinced the man to stop by her office so she could "clear her calendar for the afternoon." Her ability to remain calm and collected when things took a turn, allowed her to escape a hazardous and vulnerable situation. He definitely bit off more than he could chew! For Andy's friend, because her teachings served as a life saver, protection never tasted so sweet!

Life is about the ability to actively and intentionally shift gears. Success is on the opposite side of our comfort zone and there is a fine line between taking risks and taking calculated measures. Take enough risk to get you ahead without taking stupid risks to get you in trouble. Mitigating your losses allows you to have an increased chance for quality gains.

"All of the marketing, sales, and business training you value doesn't mean squat if you don't make it home to your family tonight." - Andy Tolbert

Shifting Gears

When opportunities present themselves, will you be willing to seize the occasion guns blazing? Will you be able to protect and preserve what you're building? Are you poised and ready to defend against the inevitable challenges in your personal and professional life? Will you be confident in the face of adversity to face your biggest enemies and live to enjoy your accomplishments? Although it could take more time and energy, are you committed to calculate, mitigate and circumstantiate your approach?

Slight shifts help you zero in on success. When you want to steer a horse, you don't yank on the reins too forcefully, but rather press lightly to gain more control. When you've been bucked, kicked and stomped in life, never give up. Saddle up and ride on!

Go after what you want with all you've got. Even though the road you travel is full of potholes and obstacles, you will have a smoother ride when your intuition, combined with exceptional self-defense training, serves as your roadside assistance. Straight roads do not make skilled drivers. Sometimes we win and sometimes we learn. Life is a one-time offer so make it count!

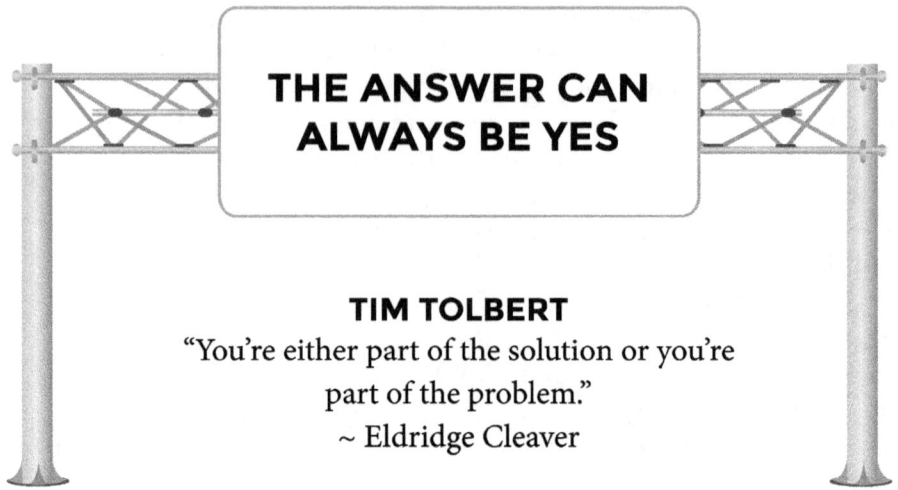

THE ANSWER CAN ALWAYS BE YES

TIM TOLBERT
"You're either part of the solution or you're part of the problem."
~ Eldridge Cleaver

Successful people take advantage of opportunities, not people. Every person and every business transaction has a unique thumbprint and our ability to serve them in their needs affords us the ability to leave a footprint on the world. When others go through experiences that cost them a fortune, solving their problems affords us the freedom to pursue our goals and dreams. The success in our past becomes the fuel to help others create victory for their futures.

A small town boy growing up in an underprivileged area in the panhandle of Florida, Tim Tolbert's father passed away when he was 6, forcing him to shift gears. "It never really goes away but time dulls the pain a little bit," Tim acknowledges.

His mother ended up marrying a Marine Corp pilot and their family was transferred to California. Eventually, his mom and step father separated. Tim's mother met her current husband, a French citizen, and they moved to France when Tim was 14. This was a huge shift because of the cultural nuances and the inevitable language barrier. When the only person who speaks English is your mother, you learn the foreign language quickly so you can converse with other people your age. Within 6 months Tim was semi-fluent and adapted well, graduating high school and gaining unique experiences. "I wouldn't trade it for anything because it was pretty cool and a whole new world for me," Tim approves.

Tim moved back to the United States to attend college at the University of Florida to pursue an aerospace engineering degree. Accustomed to a more focused studies program in France, Tim struggled with the American education curriculum that forced him to take a myriad of courses that weren't solely study specific. He discovered college wasn't the best lane for him at the time and entered the working world, leveraging his skills to get a job in the electronic sector. Eventually, he became a sales rep and took over a territory that was failing. With Tim's abilities, he doubled the territory in the first year. Unlike his competition who wore suits and ties, Tim remained true to himself and his background, donning polos and jeans as he pulled up in his Ford truck. This laid-back approach resonated with his customers better. "I wasn't the norm. I didn't look the part. I was able to meet the prospect where it made sense for them, walk right into the lab and find out exactly what they needed without a bunch of red-tape. I had to continually inform them that I didn't have the piece of paper (degree) that went with the job, which surprised them because I knew a lot more than some of the engineers because of my experience. I was able to pick up a tool and do the dirty work."

There are certain positions you must have an education for to succeed. However, from an entrepreneurial standpoint, it becomes an on-the-job degree that you learn from others and get a real-world experience, rather than a formal-education comprehension.

By taking something, looking at it inversely and going a different direction, it solved huge problems. The big picture, broken down into small frames, incrementally leads to a solution that a textbook cannot solve. When something is not working, it is often beneficial to start networking. Through healthy communication with others, it affords the opportunity to see things from a new perspective which could become the catalyst for the imperceptible answer not available in a college course.

Tim eventually got bored with the corporate world and made a shift to enter the mortgage world with his wife. "I'm not a 9-5er person. I like my flexibility and like to go on vacations with my wife and do whatever I want. I have structured my business to run from anywhere in the world." With a staunch belief that he has to know his craft inside and out, Tim essentially learned every guideline with every lender they partnered with for the first six months. He became a product of the product and knew it better than anyone. The gift was that when he started getting business he was able to handle intricate files because he knew the guidelines better than the underwriters. "If I'm going to be serving someone in the largest transaction of their life, I want to make sure I'm doing everything right," Tim professes. "And make sure they get the best deal!"

Tim epitomizes the leadership and professional qualities that every trailblazer should embody. Often, it's not just the person who works the hardest but the one who has the best interest at heart for his clients. In a corrupted world of voracity and egocentrism, Tim stood out by standing up for those who were seeking the best experience. When a lot of lenders were putting their clients into sub-prime loans, Tim's prime focus was what was best for his client. Tim became a trusted leader because of his ability to put the result and relationship above the reward. In fact, some of his most vocal "raving fans" came in the form of people he never did a loan for! If a new loan is not in your best interest, he's not afraid to tell you that.

After being in the industry for a while, Tim and his wife, Andy, decided to open their own company, which was during an overall market shift. As the correction occurred, they remained focused on service and providing the correct product for each loan. With their experience handling challenging files, they were able to grow the company successfully. They became recognized as the firm that could handle to most difficult files, making it easier to survive and become leaders while others were falling behind.

"It finally clicked. Instead of going after the same piece of pie everyone is going for, doing the perfect loan for everybody, we ended up using the knowledge of the difficult loans to our advantage." They were able to shift gears and find a unique niche with many offices as a last-ditch effort to save the files they otherwise couldn't. Other people's CAN'T became their CAN and they leveraged their expertise to salvage a lot of deals, serving the realtors and their clients, becoming a pivotal part of the buying process. They were told that they were the best when others couldn't stand up to the test.

Every time you are tempted to act in the same old way, ask if you want to be a prisoner of the past or a pioneer of the future. The easy road feels right for a moment but the difficult road will lead to the greatest reward. Straight roads don't lead to skilled drivers.

Ultimately, the bigger the risk, the bigger the reward. Entrepreneurs who own businesses are taking the risks, which afford them the potential blessings of that possibility. With that decision we each possess, comes a hierarchy of income and rightfully, the owner of the company makes significantly more than those he employs. There was a point when Tim had several friends he went to college with (who graduated by the way) working for his company. Tim is driven by the performance-based income lifestyle rather than the boxed income that is forced on him as a result of the position within a company.

The more you perfect your trade, the less you need to trade time for money.

You must make a choice to take a chance or your life will never change. Every morning we have the choice to continue sleeping with our dreams or wake up and chase them. Sometimes the wrong choices lead us to the right places while other times the right choices lead us to the wrong places. Decisions are the hardest thing to make when it is a choice between where you should be and where you want to be; unsuccessful people make choices based on their current situation and down moments, while successful people make decisions based on where they want to end up.

"When you're responsible for your income, you're also responsible for your outcomes. You put in the work to create what you want and you're building something for the future so in the future you don't have to."

Entrepreneurs reap the benefits when the market is great and the upside is limitless. The downside is your compensation is relative to performance which takes incessant internal drive and commitment.

When most got turned down, Tim and Andy got turned on to serving those who needed them most.

"Doors opened for us and we got on the right track. Our marketing budget went to zero and we didn't have to advertise. We shifted gears to go against the grain and go after the clients others couldn't serve. Our referrals were astronomical and you wouldn't believe the loyalty we gained. By changing our focus and going after those deals that had been turned down, we weren't a competition but rather a supplement," Tim recognizes.

Mutually beneficial relationships became their bread and butter and they made a lot more dough! They created a win-win-win lifestyle by exceeding the threshold most others settled for. Many people were being underserviced and Tim continually over delivered.

When we rise to the occasion and do the right things, the right opportunities arise. Tim invested his time, energy and passion into others which led him to the investment side of real estate. The incremental shift in his business gave him the confidence to shift again and enter a new division of real estate where he could leverage his knowledge and expertise. The security blanket he had built for himself was flung off when he committed to investing his own money into new assets. Tim always trusted his heart but always relied on the numbers. When you follow a proven formula and don't deviate from what works, you put the deals in place and let the numbers work for you. You need to know the rules of the game; once you do, you can create safety and mitigate loss by the way you perform to gain so much more.

Progression leads to growth, personally and in your business. Change is inevitable while progress is a choice. Even a little progress each day adds up to big results and the best way is to subtract your negative thoughts and multiply your efforts. The more you focus on what you want the more likely it is to become reality. Whatever project or goal you're working on, don't stop working on yourself.

Leaders excel in their industry's best practices and discover the voids, then fill them to become even more profitable. When you understand the shortcomings you can fix them and be in business for the long run. Tim has created unremitting success by focusing on the business he wanted to get from those who others weren't willing or able to serve. While most go after the whales, they leave the lion's share of deals for those willing to attack them. There are times to go after the windfall deals, yet other times to weather the storm you have to focus on the lowest hanging fruit.

To go the distance, you may have to drive further distances. With a focus on deals in his back yard, he was willing to go to uncharted territory. Be willing to do what others won't today so you can have what others won't tomorrow. Excuses will always be there for you, but opportunity won't. Do what the average fear and success will always be near. Tim has had a resolute, focused intention on serving those who don't get attention. When you look in directions that are underserviced and assist them purposefully, you become a leader that creates loyal followers.

With each transition, his goal has been to build a cushion that he could rely on while building up the next venture. With a realistic delayed gratification approach, Tim deliberately plans his work and works his plan. It starts with self-education and going through the motions while taking the emotions out of it and focusing on the numbers. While most ultimately experience paralysis of analysis, Tim religiously evaluates his approach; step-by-step, he takes the appropriate strides. "No education is free. You're either paying for it through money and time or getting coaching and taking classes from people who are in the business, doing what we wanted to do. When you learn through trial and error, it's usually more expensive than writing a check to a mentor. Through our success, we became the teachers and mentors, giving back and reaching more people."

Choose to take the accelerated path. With powerful mentors, you will earn as you learn; that path fast-tracks your success. Then you'll become a person of value who can mentor others and you will get to earn while helping other people learn.

Although the foundations of business are constant, sometimes the environment isn't. With both of them 100% in various aspects of the real estate industry, the market crashed really took a toll on them. All of the hard work and all of the planning was gone. They internalized the failure and looked for where they had gone wrong. One day Tim was talking to a very wealthy friend with numerous real estate holdings and he asked him what they did wrong. The friend replied "nothing, sometimes stuff just happens."

The crash impacted them hard. Not only in the short term that you could see, but overall too. For many years they shied away from investing and real estate and did just enough to get by. But a few years ago, Andy found a real estate deal that was too good to pass up and that little rental house re-kindled their passion and their vision. They've now done several transactions personally and are re-building the passive income they had before the crash. They analyze deals a little differently these days… when considering an acquisition, they ask "if the market tanks again, what's the lowest rent we think this would draw, and if we owed more than it was worth would we still want to own it?"

This shift, as with all he's faced, has made him a better entrepreneur. He uses his personal setbacks to coach his clients in structuring their transactions. He shows them what could go wrong and how to hedge against that happening. He also shows young first-time homebuyers the path to being an investor and lets their dreams take off.

Tim and Andy have created a healthy balance between their personalities and dreams. Leaders in their own ways, they discovered the road to greatness is paved better when they have a similar vision and desire to accomplish their goals. "My philosophy has always been to be straight up with people. I can sugar coat it or tell you the truth and not dance around something. My goal is to get to the root of the problem, solve it and move on. Good, bad or indifferent, my clients know they'll get the answer. Be straightforward with people and adapt your communication to whoever you are communicating with," Tim implies.

He provides valuable answers for most and it is the questions he asks that creates context to solve their problems. The night and day difference in your ability to create solutions is shedding light on the truth they may not even know is hidden. His capacity to produce unrealistic results has created a surplus for so many, even when they thought they lacked. Tim's driving focus is to get a yes for those who have gotten no's for so long. The ignorance of others becomes his desire for more knowledge so that he can provide for those who want something that they otherwise wouldn't have been granted. Tim will break his back to serve those who were being supported by someone who didn't have the spine to push hard enough on their behalf. "Somebody's mistake or inability to do their job can cost people a lifetime of expenses and heartache," Tim advises.

Success is a wide-open field, but most go through a field of land mines without a map. When you walk blindly into business, something will blow up in your face. Fortune favors the prepared. Hope is a great asset but also becomes an expensive commodity. If it is important to you, you will find a way; if not, you'll find an excuse and success occurs when your dreams are bigger than your invalidated justifications. Tim's core values have remained at the core of all his businesses. Honesty and straightforwardness are not only the keys to his clients loving him, but also serve as an elimination tool to select those he wants to service. You cannot be everything to everyone, so at least be something exceedingly meaningful to someone.

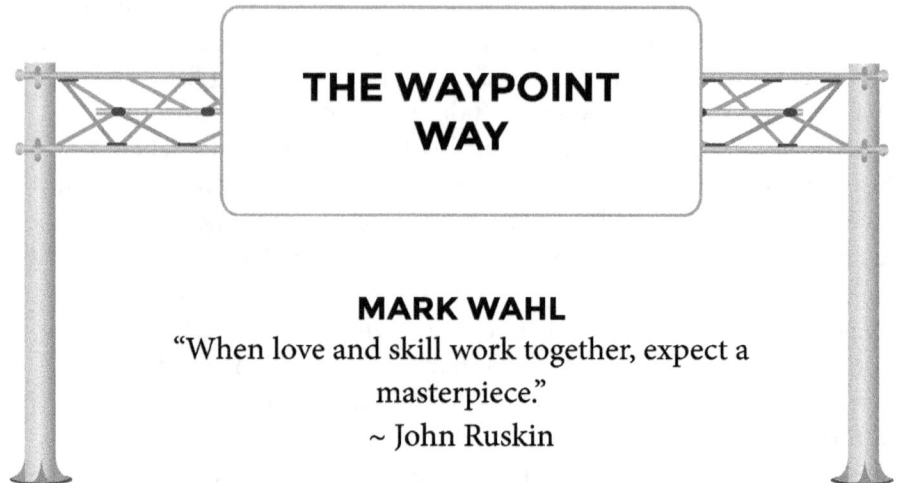

THE WAYPOINT WAY

MARK WAHL
"When love and skill work together, expect a masterpiece."
~ John Ruskin

When you walk into a room there is that one magnetic person who commands attention. Boisterous, extroverted, confident, excited about life and fun-loving, Mark Wahl has a contagious aura that attracts people to him. Successful as a business owner, loving and committed as a father, dedicated as a husband and family man and arguably, most proud and joyful as a grandfather, he is well-respected for his dynamic approach to life.

Yet, the journey to his accomplishments was not always a smooth ride. In fact, shifting gears became a part of Mark's road to success, personally and professionally.

A kid from New Jersey, Mark was ready to attack the world. Or so he thought. After attending college for 2 years, experiencing how life doesn't always go according to plan, Mark returned home on his own volition beginning a season marked by job gain and loss and no true sense of purpose.

Some people are on the right track, going the wrong way; others are on the wrong track, going the right way. Mark realized he had to shift gears and get on the right track, going the right way.

Shifting Gears

Often on the journey to self-actualization, life provides designated drivers who help us make the right turn. Mark's dad encouraged him to attend paralegal school and start working for his company. Having grown up in a family with many attorneys, Mark was intrigued and took his dad's offer.

His dad was one of the leading worker's compensation defense attorneys. While Mark obtained massive knowledge and developed important contacts, ultimately, it put a strain on the family dynamics. While he loved the job and his family, Mark was not thrilled about spending 24 hours a day with his father. Nevertheless, when we take advantage of opportunities and continue driving forward, we are often lead down new avenues.

Like a driver's test, someone can help you avoid roadblocks and help steer you toward greatness. Sometimes we should choose our own lane and other times it may be someone that helps guide us down the best path.

On the road of life, you get to determine the best speed for you. Direction is more important than speed and many end up going nowhere fast.

Mark took a step in a new direction, eventually getting in to the insurance industry where he would spend 27 years of his life. He climbed the corporate ladder from claims adjuster to regional claims supervisor for one of the largest insurance companies in the world. In the end, when you merge your best attitude with your best aptitude, you will get into the fast lane.

"There were some bumps in the road along the way," Mark admits.

One of the biggest ones was 9/11.

The top three floors of the twin towers hosted 2 of the largest insurance brokerages, and Mark had to experience 25 of his colleagues and friends perish. When the first notification on his computer popped up that a plane had crashed into the towers, he didn't give it much attention remembering other single-engine planes had hit other landmark buildings in NYC before with no real damage. When the notification popped up again for the second plane, Mark spun around in his chair and could literally see the smoke billowing from the towers from his office building that was 20 miles west of the World Trade Center. The entire world was watching them fall on television; Mark and his colleagues watched our freedom be attacked that day as the plume of smoke wafted over his office.

Emotions billowed up inside of him that day. Freedom became a lot more important to him on this landmark historical day.

"It brought back to reality what life is all about," Mark reflects. "I'm not a religious person but it certainly made me Thank God that it wasn't me or my wife because it could have been any of us."

Sometimes we feel like the Twin Towers of our lives – our finances, our relationships, our health, and our spirituality - are collapsing around us. The question is how will we rebuild? Some people waste their whole life because they are so afraid to live it; others live their whole life because they are so afraid to waste it.

Through the later years of his insurance career and moving to Florida, one of his longest and dearest friends had constantly nagged him to get into the inspection industry. His friend was on the west coast and Mark and his family had moved to the east coast to foster their family nucleus. With his corporate job and hectic travel schedule, he could barely breathe let alone think about starting his own business. Yet for a time, Mark was a corporate risk manager and spent countless hours inspecting commercial buildings and performing claim reviews. He was living in the concrete jungle but that seed of positive thought germinated and grew into a seed of opportunity. Realizing he could start building the business part-time, he traveled to the west coast and became a certified home inspector. Shortly after, he founded Waypoint Property Inspections East.

Like that seed of thought germinating, his business began growing slowly, affording him a few extra hundred dollars every week. But more importantly, it may have ultimately saved his world from collapsing around him. The totality of our abundance is measured by the ability to fulfill our dreams, utilizing our full capacity every day.

Unexpectedly, as do most lane changes, Mark was laid off from his corporate job in 2008. Emptying his office, he felt just as empty inside, too.

That same day, Mark and his wife found out that their first grandchild was going to be a boy.

When Mark placed that dreadful call to his wife to inform her he had been laid off, she was out shopping for clothes for their new grandson. Devastated, she began putting all the items back on the shelves. "You're not going to do that," Mark lovingly and optimistically commanded. "I've got Waypoint and I'm going to prove my boss wrong. I'm going to make this succeed and I will not fail at what I'm doing."

Waypoint has grown every year and is built on a solid foundation of hope, immense work ethic, quality workmanship, integrity and staff that is rooted in optimum core values.

Reflecting on his job with his father, he recognizes now that his reputation precedes him and much of it stemmed from the work ethic, quality of work, dedication, determination and commitment to success he saw in his father's business.

The transition from the corporate world to entrepreneurship is often paved with unknowns, which stop most people from ever moving forward. The road before them seems too daunting and since they cannot see the final destination, they often exit before the road that could lead to prosperity. The key is to shift gears.

"Was I scared? Absolutely. Was I nervous? Absolutely. I knew I wouldn't fail. If you're good at what you do, you believe in what you do and you have the opportunity, put your foot down and do it. When you have the chance to change lanes or shift gears, you must take the chance. There are too many regrets in life and you don't want to live your life as a regret."

Mark is devoted to making a difference in the lives of his clients. His focus has shifted from making the business successful to serving his clients above everything and trusting that through that selfless focus, Waypoint will continue to thrive. Mark wants to provide home buyers with the necessary information to make an educated decision on one of the largest purchases of their lives. They want to help realtors be more successful in their businesses. Ultimately, Mark's business is designed to ease the congestion on the road to home buying so that you can have peace of mind, while spending additional time with your family and doing the things you love most.

This drive was sparked by a flame burning in him recalling a time in his life as an assistant chef. While he loved the profession, reminiscing about his journey evoked frustrating memories recalling "the money sucked, the hours were worse and you never got to spend time with family on holidays."

Often in life and business we attempt to cook up something good but it doesn't always turn out exactly how we envisioned. Yet, like attempting to make an omelet that falls apart, you can turn it into a delicious egg scrambler.

Mark's ability to take life's challenges and turn them into prosperous lane changes is a significant key in his success. More importantly, his heart-centered approach to business is truly why Waypoint Property Inspections East is currently cooking with gas!!

The lane changes in each of our lives, those significant moments that directly or indirectly shift everything we know, help us set a new course for our ultimate destiny. After Mark had worked for his father and was happily married, as he and his wife were conversing with the family, Mark's dad turned to Mark's wife and lovingly acknowledged her. "Thank you for giving me my son back." Losing her father too early in life, Mark's wife emphasized family values and wanted to ensure that the family nucleus remained strong. Family is the lifeblood of everything important to them. The flame Mark used to cook meals provided food for the family. The flame his wife rekindled within the family provided the love that truly feeds their souls!

When Mark got engaged, planning a wedding became that much more emotionally challenging for his wife to be Jill as her father, that was everything to her, had passed away the year before. Unconventionally, yet beautifully designed, Mark's mother-in-law and soon to be daughter, walked his beautiful bride down the aisle. Since that day, she has looked upon Mark's dad to be her living father. Having someplace to go is home; having someone to love is family; having both is the greatest blessing. Family is not always blood – it's the people in your life who want you in theirs.

On the road to our greatest life, the destination we seek is only achieved by maximizing our capacity to give and contribute. The best way to do that is to follow the lane that will lead you to your greatest potential. Sometimes that means shifting gears and trusting that the road ahead will lead you to greatness. Other drivers in your life will want to instruct you on how to be happy, and yet you hold the wheel that will direct your ultimate destiny.

Waypoint, beyond the services it provides for its clients, provides so much more serving the communities they represent. From the Dolphin Cancer Challenge, Golf tournaments, to donating proceeds to Autism Awareness and the Susan G. Komen Foundation, KW Cares and Sunshine Kids and many other charities, Waypoint understands that giving back is a foundational key to success.

One day, as Mark's family was sitting around, reminiscing about life and how truly blessed they are, delving through some boxes of clothes, Mark pulled out a onesie his grandson wore as a baby. The Waypoint logo was proudly stamped on the chest and "Crawl space specialist" creatively adorned the back of the outfit. His grandson, eight years old at the time, could not believe the onesie used to fit him. Looking up at Mark, he asked when he would be able to work for the family company. Mark realized at that moment houses are made of walls and beams but what makes a home is love and dreams.

Moments like this are what drive Mark. The desire to create a lasting legacy propels his drive.

Waypoint was created by people and people are who they serve. They believe that the better role model they become as a company, the more others may look to them to become better in their own uniqueness. Waypoint is not just a company, it is a family.

"It's been a long, bumpy ride but it has ended up being a very successful ride. I hope more bumps never come but when they do we have shifted gears and changed lanes several times in life. At this point, we are in overdrive," Mark proclaims.

The journey of life is an epic expedition of self-actualization and results-driven strategic growth. Life is not about where you start or end; it is all about the distance in between. Each moment signifies a unique mile marker in our lives.

We don't always know the impact we are having on others. Always put your best foot forward. As a Lane Changer, always put the pedal to medal and do it the "Waypoint Way."

"If I can help people and have values behind it, I win," Mark confirms.

We all have different vehicles – methods and avenues for creating success - but we are all on the road of life together and can impact lives for generations to come.

The path to success is paved not just with good intentions but ethical values, hard work, patience, focus and massive action. You have been given gifts that only you can bring to the world. You have been equipped with the abilities to transform the world in ways only specifically designed for you. Perhaps it's time for each of us to inspect the foundation we are building. The landscape of the world can be changed by your willingness to transition, shift gears and take your life and business into overdrive the "Waypoint Way."

AFTERTHOUGHTS BY THE AUTHOR

Should you turn left, because nothing is going right? Or should you turn right, because you have nothing left? Life and business can feel like one big traffic jam - we have to battle stress, the challenges of building a business, the haters who doubt us along the way, "back seat drivers" who think they know better than us what we should be doing with our lives, self-doubt, constant setbacks, and perpetual roadblocks that prevent us from a smooth ride toward greatness.

Life is highway full of potholes, bumps, detours, and alternate routes. It is your choice to make the turn that leads you to your destiny. In due course, the fears we do not face become our limits. Lane Changers know the greater the change, the greater the joy. A road map gives us freedom to travel as we wish. A set of directions gives us the best route to get where we desire. In the end, it is not the places we have been that matter, but those we have yet to experience that determine our destiny. Success in life comes at the intersection of passion and massive action. When it comes to choosing a lane, most take a back seat to what they truly want and settle for what they accept, which is far less than their ultimate capability.

Perhaps it is time to buckle up and drive forward toward your true potential. We may not always see the ultimate destination, but when we keep on trucking, we can change lanes and change the course of our lives, and millions of others along the way. This is your turn. Your destination matters. You must be willing to take the wheel. Be bold on the boulevard of your dreams. Aspire to take the avenue that is best for you. Take the lane that makes you the greatest leader. Reflect on the expedition of the road that has led you where you are now. As you read each chapter from individual 'drivers' who have created massive success in their own lives, ask yourself: "How 'concrete' is my road to success?"

The driver who has already been there has valuable hindsight that could serve as your foresight. Their rearview mirror becomes your windshield. Possibly, when you finish the book, if nothing else, you look in the rear view mirror and acknowledge where you've been, is not where you want to keep going. The world is an open highway. Each of these contributors chose to take the fast lane. It may not be a road you would follow. But perhaps, just by chance, your roads cross and you can drive the world forward together. On the road to our greatest life, the destination we are seeking is only achieved by maximizing our capacity to give and contribute. In the end, when you combine your best attitude with your best aptitude, you will get into the fast lane. You hold the wheel that will direct your ultimate destiny.

Direction ultimately becomes more important than speed. Many are going nowhere fast. Some people are on the right track, going the wrong way. Others are on the wrong track, going the right way. It is time to get on the right track going the right way. The best thing in life is knowing that no matter how hard the road may get, everyone can reach their own destination in their own time. This book will ensure you are not one of the many people going nowhere recklessly! On the road of life, everything you construct starts in your mind. Make sure you remain in alignment with your core values. There will always be a high road and a low road. Few do whatever it takes to get on the high road and stay there. Go the extra mile; most people exit before then so it is a wide open road to success.

Are you ready to take the wheel and become who you want rather than who you almost could have been? This book is designed to serve as a driver's manual to help you get a tune up, to course correct where necessary for your journey, to make the essential adjustments, SHIFT GEARS, and if needed, to make an entire Lane Change. This is just the beginning. Take the principles and guidelines from the stories and implement them immediately. That, Lane Changers, is when the rubber meets the road.

THANK YOU, LANE CHANGERS

A special acknowledgment and token of gratitude to all of the contributing experts for pouring their hearts and souls into this project. Without you, it wouldn't have been conceivable. With you, anything is possible. Your selfless commitment to "Shifting Gears" serves as an illustration of how you live your lives every day. Your stories will impact so many people through this collaborative effort and your consistent effort toward your personal accomplishments is what drives the world forward. We are eternally grateful to you. YOU are the reason it will be an extremely impactful book. Together, we are creating a REVolution of Lane Changers who are "Shifting Gears" to get on the road to living their greatest lives!

AUTHOR BIOS

George Bittar

George Bittar is a real estate entrepreneur, author and has been in high impact leadership roles throughout his professional career in banking. He realized early on that experiencing true financial freedom and living life on his terms would only come by following the footsteps of his grandparents who escaped Cuba during the rise of the Castro regime and ultimately created a path to success through self-employment and calling their own shots when arriving in the United States. While George extends gratitude for the personal development and critical skills he has gained through the corporate world, his true passion is to pivot towards becoming a full-time entrepreneur and inspire others to want more out of life by reaching their highest potential and pursuing their dreams. He believes in manifesting the words of Benjamin Franklin that challenge us to "Either write something worth reading or do something worth writing." Learning to rest in the peace of God and exercising faith in action has propelled George to new heights and living life with intention.

George graduated from the New England College of Business & Finance in Boston, MA and resides in New Jersey with his loving wife Michelle and two young boys, George Jr. and Gabriel. They enjoy attending sporting events, cycling, and paying it forward by supporting organizations and causes that bring relief, hope and faith for those impacted by homelessness and poverty.

www.georgebittar.com

Jerry Gauthier

Jerry has been in banking since 2000, with TD BANK since 2005. He is very happy in his career role as an SBA Commercial Loan Officer that he has worked towards for so many years. Jerry is actively building another dream with one of his best friends in creating their own company – **Hotseat Warmers**. Currently, Jerry lives in North Jersey with his awesome wife & daughter, right next door to my brother, sister-in-law & two beautiful nieces.
Jerry.HotseatWarmers@gmail.com
www.HotseatWarmers.com

Kevin Harrington

Kevin Harrington has been a successful entrepreneur over the last 40 years. He is an Original Shark on the ABC hit, Emmy winning TV show, "Shark Tank." He is also the Inventor of the Infomercial, As Seen On TV Pioneer, Co- Founder of the Electronic Retailers Association (ERA) and Co- Founder of the Entrepreneurs' Organization (EO). Kevin has launched over 20 businesses that have grown to over $100 million in sales each, has been involved in more than a dozen public companies, and has launched over 500 products generating more than $5 billion in sales worldwide.

Kevin got his start as a young entrepreneur in the early 80's when he invested $25,000 and launched Quantum International. This turned in to a $500 million per year business on the New York Stock Exchange and drove the stock price from $1 to $20 per share. After selling his interest in Quantum International, he formed a joint Venture with the Home Shopping Network, called HSN Direct, which grew to hundreds of millions of dollars in sales. Entrepreneur Magazine has called him one of the top Entrepreneurs of our time.

The true value of Kevin is not only the 40 years of his knowledge of building businesses but also what he can do for other companies in many industries with his global Rolodex and his ability to solve problems.

To learn more about Kevin, please visit www.KevinHarrington.tv and watch this short video here: https://www.youtube.com/watch?v=5HLthP3l2_E

Jeff Hoffman

Jeff Hoffman is a successful entrepreneur, proven CEO, worldwide motivational speaker, Hollywood film producer, and a producer of a Grammy-winning jazz album in 2015. In his career, he has been the founder of multiple startups, he has been the CEO of both public and private companies, and he has served as a senior executive in many capacities. Jeff has been part of a number of well-known companies, including Priceline.com. uBid.com, CTI, ColorJar, and more.

Jeff serves on boards of companies in the US, Europe, South America, Africa, and Asia, supporting entrepreneurs and small businesses in more than 150 countries. He supports the White House, the US State Department, the United Nations, and many foreign governments on economic growth initiatives and entrepreneurship programs.

Jeff is a frequent keynote speaker, having been invited to speak in over 50 countries. He speaks on the topics of innovation, entrepreneurship, and business leadership, and is the co-author of the book SCALE, a how-to guide for growing your business. Jeff also teaches innovation workshops to major corporations on a regular basis.

Jeff is a featured business expert seen on Fox News, Fox Business, CNN, CNN International, Bloomberg News, CNBC, ABC, and NPR, and in publications including Forbes, Inc., Time, Fast Company, the Wall Street Journal, and more.

Outside of the world of technology, Jeff has produced movies, has produced musical events including concerts, tours, and charity events with such artists as Elton John, Britney Spears, NSYNC, and others, and serves on numerous charity and non-profit boards. You can email him **jeff@colorjar.com** or connect at **www.jeffhoffman.com**

Heidi Huggins

Heidi Huggins is a successful Realtor working with one of the top real estate firms in the nation. She also is working toward partnering with investors for commercial and multi-family units. After personally flipping many single family homes and working on the residential side of the market, she has learned the ins and outs of what it takes to turn a lifeless house into a beautiful place a family can call home. Wanting to always go to the next level, she is venturing into commercial investments properties from emerging markets.

Heidi is married to her business partner Scott. They have 6 handsome boys, a beautiful daughter, and an amazing grandson. When she is not working Heidi is taking trips with Scott to meet successful people that are influential and have ideas or theories about enterprise. Also, she is seeking out education for the commercial business side. She enjoys traveling the world going to conferences and non-profit events. She also makes specialty cakes for weddings, birthdays, and other special events for fun.

Heidi has a heart for mentoring people and meeting their needs. She loves to give, share, and create an atmosphere of positive influence. Heidi's vision is to tell her story all over the world and become a life-changing speaker and coach. "The most rewarding part of leadership is to serve. I have to give back because so much has been given and given back to me."

Scott Huggins

Scott Huggins is an avid leader and influencer in the real estate community. He works with some of the top real estate professionals and investors in the industry to acquire investment and multifamily apartment communities in emerging markets across the US. Scott is passionate about exchanging ideas to help others obtain their dreams and improve their lives. In his free time Scott loves to travel with his family. He also loves to teach and works with several organizations to impact and change the lives of others. You can connect with Scott at **scott@theapartmentinvestors.com**.

Justin Lofton

Facebook advertising and business acceleration expert, Justin Lofton is the founder and CEO of Zenfusion and SyncSumo. Just has a passion to help others leverage Facebook ads to grow their business. He's spent nearly 20 years mastering the art of selling online across every industry and channel imaginable.

Justin has spent more than $10M on Facebook's ad platform over the past six years while growing his agency Zenfusion, his SaaS company SyncSumo and several of his own multi-million dollar ecommerce brands.

Benita Oliver

Benita Oliver resides in San Diego, California. She loves to travel, play volleyball, kayak and help others in need. You can connect with her on Facebook, LinkedIn or Instagram. "I am passionate about helping people find their niche in life and helping companies succeed to the next level. It's all about shifting gears!"

Paul Oster

Paul Oster, FICO Pro is considered the "Nation's Credit Repairman". A credit expert who has appeared on numerous network radio and TV shows (FOX BUSINESS NEWS, CBS, ABC, NBC, FOX, PIX11). He has also written for Kiplinger's, WSJ, and the Daily News. Mr. Oster is the founder and President of Better Qualified, LLC. Paul has over 20 years of experience in both the insurance and banking industries and, has dedicated his life as a consumer advocate. Paul is also proud to serve on the Board of Directors for the American Red Cross. His humor and intelligence are highly sought-after from executives in the C-Suite of major corporations.

Lauren Ranes

The coast is close to home and heart rooted for this native Californian. Lauren can be found by the palm trees near the ocean, fanning the flames of health, happiness, and excellence. Always doing her best to make every day a great day by cherishing each moment of living an overflowing life. Extensive education of health and nutrition in addition to versatile life and experience, contributes to Lauren's unique approach to holistic healing in relation to lifestyle and image for the body and soul.

Lauren is passionate about inspiring the personal awareness and development of the people she considers herself blessed to spend time and work with. Lauren's primary focus, both professionally and personally, combines experiential education, intimate advocacy, and extraordinary adventures to create tenacious exploration of personal development and awareness.

Every day is an experience, any day can be an adventure! For more information about Lauren, to get involved, or to experience your next excellent adventure in health visit tenaciousexploration.com.

Andy Tolbert

My career in the real estate industry started in 1995 but my journey to an awareness of my own safety and of those around me has probably been a part of my life since I was a young child when our family business was the target of an armed robbery.

All of us have certain "stories" that go through life with us. Sometimes they serve us and help us move forward and sometimes they hinder and hold us back. These same stories can either save our life or paint a giant red target on our back. Once we realize which is which, we are better in a position to recognize threats and opportunities and finally take control of our life, business, and happiness.

When I teach a safety class I take on many roles in my student's life... bodyguard, marketing consultant, life coach, and sometimes therapist. In the short 2-4 hours I have their attention, I know that their life may literally depend on my ability to show them the importance of safety protocols, but also how to implement them simply and affordably into their day to day life.

I'm a real estate broker, loan officer, instructor and investor as well as a self-defense and firearms instructor. I'm also the world Wii Champion (in my house at least) and my alter-ego/Mii "Bad Andy" sometimes teaches the lessons you may not want to hear. I'm married to Tim and we have 2 dogs. We live down by the river in Central Florida and I love seeing the wildlife every day including turkeys, bear, deer, and even manatees and gators!

I'm super easy to find on social media... follow us on Facebook & Instagram @saferagent

Or reach out to us at **www.SaferAgent.com**

Tim Tolbert

Redneck Financial Expert, is that a thing? Well it is now! My country roots show strong… loyalty, integrity, honesty… those are a given where I'm from. Unfortunately, these traits aren't so common in the real estate world, and especially in my field as a mortgage broker.
I'm an engineering-brain by nature and tend to analyze everything, which is great for my clients. I've set up my business to run from anywhere in the world, and might even be found in a tree stand underwriting a loan file.
My wife, Andy, and I enjoy traveling, being on the water, and competitive shooting (we're not going to win any medals but we have fun). When I'm not helping someone finance the home of their dreams or showing them how to invest for passive income, I enjoy any time I can get in the outdoors. Look closely and you might see me cameo in a TV show or film, but don't blink!
Find me on Facebook or **www.TimTolbert.com**

Mark Wahl

Mark Wahl is the Owner/General Manager of Waypoint Property Inspections East, LLC, which was established in 2006. After being in corporate America for more than 20 years, he has been highly motivated to build a very successful business. Mark was raised in New Jersey and moved to South Florida in 2005. He is a devoted husband, dad and grandfather to his wife Jill, daughter Meridith and his grandchildren Landon, Liam and Lizzy.
Contact Mark personally
561.676.0546
www.waypointeast.com

Changing Lanes International will help you find success when life shifts. Our mission is not to change people; it's to give them the ability to change what they need in order to change their path to absolute abundance. We want you to be a part of the Changing Lanes community so we can impact the world in a greater way. You are a Lane Changer.

Accelerate. Your. Dreams.

Ready to write your own book? Connect at
www.PaveYourOwnLane.com
Want to be a bestselling author with Changing Lanes International? Email **info@ChangingLanesNOW.com** today and learn how to participate in an upcoming collaboration.
You can also visit us at: **www.ChangingLanesInternational.com**

Want a 90-day game plan to accelerate your dreams and get your business into the fast lane? Go to **www.ChangingLanesInternational.com** to get your FREE consultation!

Lane Ethridge is the Founder & CEO of Changing Lanes International. He is a phenomenal visionary, a creative marketer and an international speaker. He built a business around empowering entrepreneurs to maximize their gifts and skills to drive their business forward. He is a communication master and helps you craft your message to create millions. Lane has the unparalleled ability to take your story and help you turn it into a signature keynote.
Changing Lanes International helps entrepreneurs increase their Recognition (Visibility), AUTHORity (Credibility) and Collaborative Contribution (Philanthropic Value Proposition) so that you can maximize your efforts to raise your value in the marketplace, allowing you to increase the cost for your services.
He teaches you the skills to empower others and leverage your uniqueness for captivating new prospects and acquiring new clients. As a 4x #1 bestselling author he turns you from an author to an AUTHORity! Together, we will help define your lane, build your overall brand to monetize most effectively and increase the size of your digital footprint to maximize your global reach and impact.
Lane is also a successful real estate investor. On the road to personal financial success, he is building an empire, and since he never gives up, his drive and success affords him the ability to constantly give back.

Shifting Gears

www.ingramcontent.com/pod-product-compliance
Lightning Source LLC
Chambersburg PA
CBHW070249230526
45470CB00002B/537